STONE OF DESTINY

STONE OF DESTINY

PAT GERBER

PHOTOGRAPHS BY ANDREW MORRIS

CANONGATE

First published in Great Britain in
1997 by Canongate Books Ltd,
14 High Street, Edinburgh

New Edition 1997

ISBN 0 86241 670 1

HB ISBN 0 86241 721 X (U.S.A)

British Library Cataloguing-in-publication Data
A catalogue record for this book is available
on request from the British Library

Typeset by Hewer Text Composition Services, Edinburgh
Printed and bound in Finland by WSOY

CONTENTS

Acknowledgements   vii
Introduction   xi

 1 Carried Away at Christmas   1
 2 The Hostage Stone   12
 3 Queens, Kings and Coronation Chairs   22
 4 How the Legends Began   28
 5 Jacob and the Thunder Stones   41
 6 Ireland   47
 7 Romans and Christians   53
 8 Dalriada and the Royal Boar   62
 9 Columba, King of Storms   68
10 Dunstaffnage   79
11 Scotland United   84
12 Who Owns Scotland?   90
13 England's Edward and the Celtic Fringes   97
14 Robert the Bruce   107
15 The Stone of Skye   118
16 The Knights Templar   129
17 Sir Walter Scott and Edinburgh Castle   134
18 Macbeth's Castle   140
19 A Royal Peculiar   151
20 Back to the Future   160
21 The Stone of Destiny   174
22 Freedom Come-All-Ye   182

Chronology   192
Sources   195
Index   199

ACKNOWLEDGEMENTS

Many people and institutions have helped in the making of this book. We are deeply grateful to all of them, in particular to: Professor Leslie and Elizabeth Alcock, Donald Anderson, *Arbroath Herald*, Argyll Estates, Norman Atkinson, BBC Radio Scotland, Professor G. Barrow, Catriona and Donald Bell, Jimmy Blain, British Library, British Museum, British Newspaper Library, Ian Brown, Buckingham Palace, Dr David Caldwell, Alastair Campbell of Airds, Ann and Peter Campbell, Danny Campbell, Bill Cameron, Bryony Carnie, Christopher Carnie, Jamie Carnie, Patrick Carnie, Penny Carnie, Clan Donald Centre, Professor Edward Cowan, Catherine Crufts, Alastair J. Cuthbert, Clifford J. Denovan, Donald Dewar MP, Professor A.A.M. Duncan, Dundee Art Galleries and Museums, Dr Graham Durant, Neil Dougan, Joan Earle, Eileen Eaton, Gillian Eatough, Edinburgh Castle, Professor A. Fenton, Marion C. Fentum, Finlaggan Trust, Ian Finlay, Flt Lt David Gale, Cyril Gerber, Ian Hamilton QC, Margaret Harrison, Dr Hamish Henderson, P.H. Henderson, *Herald* and *Evening Times* Picture Library, HMSO, Dr Peter Hill, Sue Hillman, Historic Scotland, Jim Hume, the India Office Library, the Iona Community, Jordanhill College Library, Arnold Kemp, Dr Lawrence Keppie, Elspeth King, Gordon Leslie, Janice Lindsay, Dr E. Mairi MacArthur, Ian Macdonald QC, Sir Ian Bosville Macdonald of Sleat, Margaret Macdonald, Robert Macdonald, Sweyn Macdonald, Revd Uist Macdonald, Dr Norman Macdougall, Jimmie MacGregor, Sheila McGregor, Stuart McHardy, Lorn MacIntyre, Mhairi McIntyre, Ishbel McKenzie, Rona and Donald McKenzie, Archie McKerracher, Angus McKinnon, Dr Alasdair Maclean,

B. Macleod, Bert McNulty, Professor John MacQueen, Lady Pamela Mansfield, Robyn Marsack, Elizabeth Marshall, Kay Matheson, Meigle Museum, A. Minty, Mitchell Library, Lady Naomi Mitchison, Professor Rosalind Mitchison, Alistair Moffat, Montrose Museum, Ronald W. B. Morris, the National Library of Scotland, the National Museums of Scotland, Norman Newton, Revd John Mackay Nimmo, Sir Iain Noble, the People's Palace, Christine Primrose, Erina Rayner, Christine Reynolds, School of Scottish Studies, Scone Palace, *Scotsman*, Scottish Record Office, Scottish Television, George Shepherd, Jim Sillars MP, Jamie Sinclair, George Smith, Somerset House, Harry Stanger Ltd, Emma St John-Smith, David Stewart, Alan Stuart, Ronald Stuart, Lisbeth M. Thoms, Nigel Tranter, University of Glasgow, University of Edinburgh, University of St Andrews, Margaret Walker, Dr Fiona Watson, Whithorn Trust, Rob Welsh, Westminster Abbey, Margaret Wilson, Brian Wilton, Daphne and George Wyllie, Sue Youngs.

We are grateful to the following for permission to use illustrations: *Herald*, HMSO, Historic Scotland, The Hunterian Museum, Dr Graham Durant, Ronald Morris, Mairi MacArthur, *Scottish Daily Express*, the *Sunday Mail*, the *Sunday Post*, D. C. Thomson.

THE WEE MAGIC STANE

O the Dean o' Westminster wis a powerful man
He held a' the strings o' the State in his hand
And a' this great power it flustered him nane
Til some rogues ran away wi' his wee magic stane.
Wi a tooreli ooreli ooreli ay etc.

Noo the stane had great powers that could dae such a thing
For withoot it it seemed we'd be wantin' a king.
So he called in the polis and gave this decree
Go and hunt oot the stane and return it tae me.

So the polis went keekling way up tae the north
They hunted the Clyde and they hunted the Forth,
But the wild folk up yonder just pitied them a'
For they didnae believe it wis magic at a'.

Noo the Provost o' Glesga Sir Victor by name
He was very pit oot when he heard o' the stane,
So he offered the statues that stand in George Square
That the High Churches might mak a few mair.

When the Dean of Westminster with this wis acquent
He sent for Sir Victor and made him a saint.
'But it's no use you sending your statues down heah'
Said the Dean, 'but you've given me a jolly good idea.'

So he quarried a stane o' the very same stuff
And he dressed it all up till it looked like enough,
Then he sent for the press and announced that the stane
Had been found and returned tae Westminster again.

When the thieves found out what Westminster had done
They ran aboot diggin' up stanes by the ton
And for each one they finished they entered the claim
That this wis the real and original Stane.

But the cream o' the joke still remains tae be tellt
Fur the bloke that wis turnin' them aff on the belt
At the peak o' production wis sae sorely pressed
That the real yin got bunged in alang wi' the rest.

So if ever ye come on a Stane wi' a ring
Just sit yersel' doon and proclaim yersel' King.
For there's nane wid be able tae challenge yer claim
That ye'd crowned yersel' King on the Destiny Stane.

Johnny McEvoy.

INTRODUCTION

W hat is the Stone of Destiny? Is it the flat sandstone block which was brought to Edinburgh amidst much pomp and panoply one St Andrew's Day, or is it really something more like the ghost of Scotland's past, a strangely fascinating realisation of myth and legend? Why do archaeologists and ordinary folk keep hunting for it in the castles, lochs, mountainsides, rivers and bogs of Scotland, and what exactly is it they hope to find?

Stone stories are part of Scottish culture. The first reappearance of the Coronation Stone north of the border in 1951 generated strong feelings in Scots around the globe. Its more ceremonial arrival in 1996 engendered different emotions in the watching crowd.

How did the Stone of Destiny come to be lost? Edward I of England came raging through the land in 1296. He wanted to root out the source of Scotland's strength, to weaken Scots' morale. He believed he stole away our most important talisman: we believe he was palmed off with a fake. But his unprecedented cruelties still haunt the relationship between Scotland and England, in spite of all manner of treaties of union. And that relationship affects every single person living and working in Scotland today.

There are those who feel it's risky to examine openly the differences between the two nations; if we dare to trace the treatment which has been meted out to a piece of our rock, let alone to the actual people, do we invite bloody revolution?

The context in which we live matters to us. The experience of growing up and working in Glasgow, Scotland, is quite different from that of growing up and working in Ireland,

Israel or India, in spite of our common humanity. Our folk memories are part of the package which marks each of us as an individual. If for some reason we lose touch with our past, through displacement, accident or amnesia, we lose a part of ourselves. Folk traditions are taught in schools precisely to help children identify, not only with the cultures from which they come, but also with that in which they are growing up. At the very least we have a natural curiosity about our parents, an emotional bond whether it be hate or love for the place in which we spent our childhoods, and a feeling of community with the race or races from which we originate – and their folklore.

Is there precedent, anywhere in the world, for a stone being venerated in quite the same way as the Stone of Destiny, and for such a long time? Why is it that we, people of late twentieth century Europe – sophisticated, materialistic as never before – are still so fascinated by magic?

The Stone of Destiny has intrigued story-tellers from Miss Jane Porter and her contemporary Sir Walter Scott to twentieth-century novelists such as Compton Mackenzie and Nigel Tranter. It has even turned up in science fiction, thanks to American Patricia Kennealy who linked the story with Arthurian legend in her novel *The Throne of Scone* (1986).

In recent times legends have been kept for children, along with fairytales but, in view of the mass destruction of documentary evidence in Scotland caused by fire, pillage, 'rescue', mildew and Reform, our historians have evolved new routes into the past, one of which is through folklore.

The legend of the Stone of Destiny links into other Scottish traditions – the Loch Ness Monster, even the doings of Lancelot and Guinevere – which shadow the movement of people and ideas through the Dark Ages till they arrive in the daylight of the present century.

The English antiquarian Thomas Pennant (1726–98) was one of Scotland's early tourists. He provides the first full written story about the Stone of Destiny. He writes when at Scone:

> In the church of the abbey was preserved the famous chair, whose bottom was the fatal stone, the palladium of the Scottish monarchy; the stone, which had first served Jacob for his pillow, was afterwards transported into Spain, where it was used as a seat of justice by Gethalus, contemporary with Moses. It afterwards found its way to Dunstaffnage in Argyllshire, continued there as the Coronation Chair till the reign of Kenneth II, who, to secure his empire, removed it to Scone. There it remained, and in it every Scottish monarch was inaugurated till the year 1296, when Edward I, to the mortification of North Britain, translated it to Westminster Abbey, and with it, according to ancient prophecy, the empire of Scotland.

To whom does the Stone matter today? The answer lies, as we shall see, in the actions of those who believe they have had it in their keeping. So important is it to the monarchy, to the established Church of England, and to the people of Britain, that it is kept corralled in the most effective security system human ingenuity can devise – in case its essence escapes? Or because possession is all?

Several other stones are kept under conditions of tight security in Scotland. The hiding-place of a Hebridean Stone is handed down only from father to son – we are not told what happens if the heir is a daughter. Anonymous letter-writers tell of Stones scattered over the landscapes of Scotland like raisins in a scone. There are mystics, ministers, lords and lay-people who know of the whereabouts of other stones, and who will tell, when the time is ripe. Scul?tor George Wyllie has a tendency to mix his own Carry-out Stones.

The legends to which we are the heirs overlap and contradict each other. They are riddled with tantalising gaps over which writers have taken colossal imaginative leaps – which is how new stories begin. Nevertheless, we shall set out bravely to attempt a closer look. What sources can we tap? Where is the thin fabric of fact patched with wishful thinking? The main thread of the story, as related by Pennant, comes from some of the earliest known writings of Homo Sapiens, and perhaps even from the exploding of some comet in outer space. It winds along the routes of tribal movement from Israel to Egypt, Greece, Spain, up the western coast of France to Brittany, Ireland and thence to Scotland. All the tales come together at Scone in the tenth century, then fray out into yet more, ranging from Islay, Iona and Skye, across the breadth of Perthshire, to Edinburgh Castle, from Whithorn and Melrose in the borders to the shores of the Moray Firth and even, some say, as far as the shores of Nova Scotia.

Was Scota an ancestor of the present queen? What made Scota want to voyage to the damp and chilly north? Why did Nennius bother to write her story? Why did Columba follow Jacob's fad for sleeping on stone pillows? Exactly what is it that makes a royal personage need to lower her posterior on to a small and undistinguished-looking slab of Perthshire sandstone in public, before she can truly feel Queen of the United Kingdom?

Some questions may prove unanswerable, given the present state of knowledge and the limitations of the writer, but it is hoped that the reader, whether erudite or merely curious, will find this book interesting, and perhaps even useful as a starting-point for further researches, and that a platform will have been built for discussion and debate.

Several people in Scotland are currently taking an interest in the whereabouts of the Stone, and have kindly offered the fruits of their research. The information collected comes from the work of story-tellers, archaeologists, song-writers, historians, farmers, churchmen, sculptors, genealogists, journalists, kings, advocates, seers, accountants, knights, academics, dreamers, aristocrats, teachers, travellers, politicians and poets. Letters and phone-calls have come not only from Scottish addresses, but also from England, Canada, the United States, Africa, Australia and New Zealand. Clearly there must be some truth in the belief that, although there may be fewer than 5,000,000 people in Scotland, the world as a whole is the richer by an estimated 90,000,000 émigré Scots.

Folk-tales have a kinetic energy of their own. In writing them down, one risks making them too definite, incapable of re-interpretation. Duncan Williamson, the Traveller-story-teller, permits his stories to be published reluctantly, feeling that the process of writing can kill a story dead so that it becomes nothing more than a specimen for scientific inspection, like a pinned butterfly. A real tale *should* be free to move, according to the mood of the day, the audience, the time of year. Each nation once had its own oral tradition, its folklore handed down, like the old game of Whispers, to grow and fade, mutate, and live again in every telling.

In order that you be free to make up your own mind about the Stone, or indeed Stones, based on your own particular reactions, your knowledge, your interests, biases and perceptions, the evidence is presented as often as possible in its raw state for your consideration.

We now embark on a journey through time and space where all the routes converge on Scotland, and from which they disperse, leaving mysterious trails as vague as the mountain mists, as colourful and as changing as October rainbows on the Sound of Sleat.

≈

CHAPTER ONE

CARRIED AWAY AT CHRISTMAS

The Coronation Stone has been returned to Scotland after 700 years of exile. This time it comes with the blessing of Her Majesty the Queen and her Secretary of State for Scotland, Michael Forsyth, but perhaps it is best known for its earlier secret journey across the border after four students spirited it out of Westminster Abbey on Christmas morning 1950.

Their adventures have been documented in the autobiographies of one of the protagonists, Ian Hamilton, and we begin with a glance at that event in order to see it in its historical context.

The history of the Coronation Stone begins in 1296 when the English king Edward I seized what he believed was the ancient Stone of Destiny from Scone, Perthshire, and had it sent to Westminster Abbey. After the Act of Union with England in 1707, Scotland was able to develop both intellectually and spiritually, producing the great thinkers of the Enlightenment and writers such as Robert Burns, James Hogg and Sir Walter Scott. A renewal of interest in itself as a nation arose, and the imprisonment of the Stone became, for some, a symbol of England's repression of the people of Scotland.

Thanks partly to Scott's historical novels, by the late nineteenth century this feeling gave rise to a series of plots to bring the Stone back. The first of these proved unsuccessful, but the attempts appealed to the Scots' sense of humour and received wide press coverage, encouraging discussion of Home Rule and keeping the topic on the boil. In 1886 a Counsellor at Law, Eric Macdonald Lockhart, published a pamphlet in which he wrote: 'There has been a growing up of *Centralisation* in Westminster, and a movement in the opposite direction is now very much required.' He went on: 'If the truth must be told, Scotland has never occupied her own proper place in the councils of the Nation, since the Union was scandalously carried through.' Lockhart advocated federal union between the nations of Britain, and self-government for Scotland.

In the twentieth century, between two terrible wars, leading Scottish thinkers continued the debate. They looked for ways to stir Scots up sufficiently to effect the political changes they wanted. It was very hard to do. The attitude of the Scottish people remains sceptical: politicians and those in power are deemed untrustworthy, ordinary folk remain powerless – what is the point of voting when it fails to change anything? So they shrug their shoulders and get on with their lives.

Activists wishing to counteract this attitude thought, all right, if we can't fire people's imagination with talk, let's try making them laugh – and while laughing they might just open their minds for long enough to listen to our ideas and begin to believe that change is possible.

Several factors came together to fix the idea of bringing the Coronation Stone home in the minds of certain individuals. In *The North Wind Of Love* (1944), Compton MacKenzie wrote of his plot to rescue it on St Andrew's Day 1932. Nigel Tranter has an English research team digging up the one Edward I supposedly failed to find, forcing questions about it into the open, in his recently reprinted novel *The Stone* (1958). Clearly both authors perceived the captive Stone as a symbol of the subjugated Scottish people. Poet Hugh MacDiarmid supported the cause, but actor Duncan MacRae involved himself in an actual attempt to take the Stone, when the first replica stone was cut, intended as a replacement while the conspirators got away with the original. Their plan failed. Robert (Bertie) Gray, a monumental sculptor in Glasgow, kept the replica in his yard for many years, and more copies may have been made later.

Scottish service personnel coming home from war in the late 1940s, having seen their friends killed and maimed in the name of Democracy, believed Scotland had come of age, had won the right to demand reform. Some disseminated their ideas at universities, and those of us still at school picked up the excitement and went fly-posting and slogan-painting at night.

The Labour government proved uninterested in the failing economies of the north, and the tiny Scottish National Party hadn't yet caught on. But in November 1949 a Glasgow lawyer, Dr John MacCormick, launched the Scottish Covenant, which had more moderate ideals than the SNP. Members sought reform and self-government, but remained loyal to the Crown. On a tidal wave of optimism MacCormick was elected Rector of Glasgow University, and by June 1950 a seventh of the Scottish electorate had joined the Covenant movement. Hundreds of students thirled themselves to the cause, including Kay Matheson, Ian Hamilton, Gavin Vernon and Alan Stuart.

That year Churchill's party was returned to power and Scotland was in effect disenfranchised. Ian Hamilton, studying Law at Glasgow University, decided something had to be done and, when he met Kay at a Covenant party that October, found her in a similar frame of mind.

Kay, a trainee teacher, was born in Inverasdale, Rosshire, 'the year the Scottish National Party was formed', December 1928. A small, gently-spoken woman with a wry sense of humour, preferring Gaelic to English, she looks directly at you, taking time to think before she speaks; 'I'm still hoping that we will get self-government.' She found Hamilton arrogant, but liked his enthusiasm and commitment. Hamilton remembers her ethereal quality – she was as 'remote as a Hebridean island'.

Three years her senior, slightly built himself, highly intel-ligent and a bit of a loner, Hamilton had been a nationalist since his schooldays. He believed Parliament must pay heed to the serious requests coming from Scotland. Otherwise frustration would erupt into violence, for militancy was in the air. Westminster had greeted the Scottish Covenant with the collective yawn it reserved for the lunacies of the Celtic fringe. The whingeing Scots, as irritating as their own midges, were complaining again. Politicians had more important things to attend to. Hamilton thought if only he could succeed in bringing the Stone back to Scotland it would be a symbolic, political and bloodless gesture. To achieve this he was prepared to risk jail and the wreckage of his legal career. It simply did not occur to him that people might write off the escapade as a student prank.

In September 1950 he reconnoitered Westminster Abbey. Back in Glasgow he researched in the Mitchell library. He decided to make his attempt in the Christmas break. He needed a car, money, burglar's tools and confederates. Whom could he trust? Financial backing to the tune of ten pounds came from a Glasgow businessman who had been involved in the 1930s' attempt. Bertie Gray, not only a monumental sculptor but also a Glasgow Councillor and Vice-Chairman of the Covenant, produced the replica stone from his Lambhill store.

At the end of every Michaelmas Term, Glasgow University holds an all-night ball known as Daft Friday. Kay Matheson accompanied Ian Hamilton, who told her his plans and suggested she become involved. She was discreet. Nobody would suspect such a pretty girl, the innocence shining out of her.

Kay thought he was pulling her leg. She listed those who had failed – Wendy Wood, Hugh MacDiarmid, John MacCormick himself. What made Ian think he'd succeed? He told her. She says 'I suppose I was the obvious choice. I wasn't a nervous sort of person – and I could drive. They thought a lassie would not be suspected, and that I might be more likely to bring the Stone back to Scotland safely than a man would.'

They recruited Gavin Vernon, an easy-going student, and planned their journey. But on the afternoon of Friday 22nd December, when they went to collect Gavin, he had a friend with him: Alan Stuart, offering a second car, was desperate to help. Deciding it was safer to take him than to leave

4

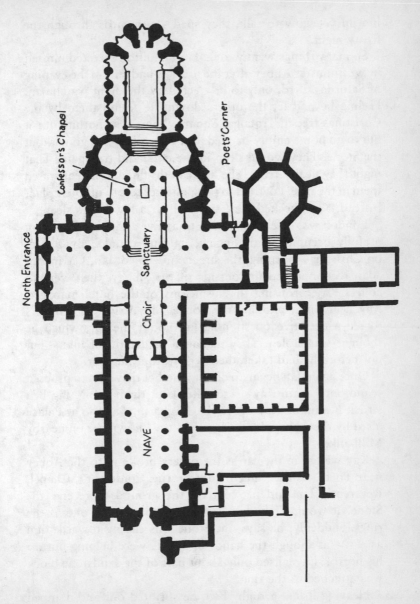

Plan of Westminster Abbey

him in Glasgow to talk, they sped southwards through the frosty night.

So many things went wrong. Ian Hamilton secreted himself in Westminster Abbey after the tourists had left on the evening of Saturday 23rd, only to be ejected by the night watchman. Feeling he had let the others down, he found them by the Christmas tree in Trafalgar Square. There was nothing for it but to go home empty-handed. But Kay refused to go without the Stone. They would sleep in the cars, and try again. That night they nearly froze. She had caught flu, and defeat stared them in the face. Ian tried to persuade her to call off their plan. Instead, Kay checked in at an hotel for a few hours sleep.

London was celebrating Christmas Eve and the police were usefully occupied with singing, fighting drunks. By 2 a.m. on Christmas morning, the streets quietened. Ian, Gavin and Alan reconnoitered the outside of the Abbey, then went to collect Kay, arousing the suspicions of the hotel manager. Kay heard him phoning the police. She arrived downstairs to see a detective questioning Ian about the car, which he thought was stolen. They managed to get rid of him – but not before he had taken their registration number.

Once again Ian began to doubt whether they should proceed – and once again Kay's resolution kept them going. Big Ben struck 4 a.m. as Kay drove the Anglia into a lane at Palace Yard by the Abbey. Ian had parked the known car on nearby Millbank.

Kay waited in the car as the others broke in to the Abbey near Poets' Corner and made for the Confessor's Chapel. Reverently Ian laid his coat on the ground to receive the Stone. It wouldn't budge. Tentatively, he pulled one of the rings. Suddenly, he says, the Stone was sliding towards him as easily as though the hands of angels were helping but, to his horror, he realised only about half of the sandstone block was attached to the ring.

Heaving it like a rugby ball, he sprinted out and dumped the lump of stone in the Anglia. Dashing back, he helped manoeuvre the larger half onto his coat. The three had just started to slide it towards the door when they heard Kay start the car. Ian ran out again, to leap into the passenger seat. What was she thinking about? They weren't ready to leave yet. Kay whispered, 'A policeman is coming towards us' and promptly melted into Ian's arms.

So affected was the constable by the young lovers that he spent time kindly explaining where they could find a darker car-park. He also divulged that no bobby would be keen to make an arrest that night, for he wouldn't want to spend Boxing Day in Court. But when he left they knew the Anglia's number was also now on record. Kay decided to get her part of the Stone out of London immediately. 'We didn't break it, you know. It had been cracked by a suffragette's bomb.'

A traffic light stopped her outside Harrods in Knightsbridge. When she started off again there was a loud thump. She pulled in. 'Ian hadn't closed the boot properly, and the Stone landed in the middle of the road. I had to lift it back in again. I had the muscle, from carrying the peats – I probably had more muscle than Ian did at that time.'

Mary Chalk, a Birmingham girl, shared digs with Kay in Glasgow. Birmingham would be a convenient first stop. Although somewhat surprised to see Kay, Mary gave her a welcome, a good dark garage for the Anglia, and a credulous ear for her cooked-up story. The Chalk family were expecting a guest for Christmas lunch. He turned out to be the Chief Constable of Birmingham.

'It wasn't funny at the time,' says Kay. 'When he came in I thought they had discovered everything.' But she kept her nerve, fighting off fatigue and the encroaching flu, keeping the Chief Constable's mind off his work by playing party games with him. When the lunchtime news came over the radio, announcing the disappearance of the Stone, 'The paper hat nearly flew off my head. But he never suspected a thing. Well then the news was out. The border roads were closed, for the first time in four hundred years. So I went and stayed with another friend in Scarborough. She was delighted to keep me until the borders were opened again.'

As soon as it was safe to travel Kay made her way north to her mother in Inverasdale, after her Christmas 'holiday'. The Anglia and its cargo remained hidden in the Birmingham garage.

Meanwhile Ian, who had collected the spare car from Millbank and driven back to the Abbey, discovered that Gavin and Alan had vanished. End-over-end, single-handed, he heaved the Stone out and on to the back seat. 'I think it went quite easily . . . the hands of God were over mine.' Then, filled with wild elation, he drove southwards. This was a good idea, for the police would obviously block all roads north, but how do you know which way is south, in an unfamiliar town, in the dark? When dawn came he was still being misdirected around London by strangers. Suddenly he spotted Gavin and Alan, walking along a road.

Gavin was told to wait while Ian and Alan sped towards Kent, where they planked the Stone on a grassy bank. They returned to Westminster, where Ian retrieved his coat, worrying about what his father, a Paisley tailor, would say about the dreadful state he had got it into. Through that frosty night they returned to Kent, collected the Stone, and searched for a better hiding-place. At the edge of a wood by an airfield near Rochester, they hollowed out a hiding-place in some scrubby grass. The Stone should be safe there. Expecting arrest at any moment, they posted a rough map of the Stone's hiding-place to friends in Glasgow, and headed north.

They got as far as Doncaster before the police stopped them. Had they seen the Coronation Stone? Ian said firmly that it should have been taken back to Scotland years ago. Stifling a yawn, the policeman waved them on. That night, very late and very exhausted, they reached the Stuarts' Barrhead home, a warm welcome and a whisky apiece.

Alan's father was a builder. He told them that the Stone, after six dry centuries in the Abbey, might now be soaking up dampness by day and splitting into frosted crumbs by night. Gavin joked about shovelling it into paper pokes to bring it home. Bertie Gray reassured them but Ian, who genuinely revered the Stone, blamed himself for putting it at risk.

The worst thing was not knowing how much the police knew: surely Scotland Yard must have some information? Were they being watched? How could they retrieve the Stone before Scotland Yard caught up with them?

Kay invited Alan to spend New Year at Inverasdale, but it was not to be. Late in December, leaving Bertie Gray to deliver an anonymous petition to the press, Alan and Ian set off south in the Stuart family's large Armstrong-Siddeley. The AA warned of blizzards to come as the pair drove down frozen roads on packed snow, with two new helpers. Johnny Josselyn was 'a strange, wild, brilliant character'. He was an Englishman working for the Admiralty in Bath, who had been educated in Scotland and was a strong Scotophile. Bill Craig, President of Glasgow University Union, had been unable to go with them on the first journey. The weather slowed them and they didn't reach London till the following night. At a cafe they read a headline in the *Star*: 'STONE: ARRESTS EXPECTED SOON'. Were they driving straight into an ambush?

They had few choices. To go home without the Stone and risk its disintegration? Or to go on towards Rochester and risk capture?

Once in Kent they began to recognise landmarks. But when they reached the place where they thought they'd hidden the Stone, they saw only the flickering flames of a gypsies' bonfire. They drove on.

They came back. The gypsies were encamped exactly on the spot where the Stone lay.

It was too much of a coincidence. The 'gypsies' could only be the CID in fancy dress, waiting to pounce. The idea of policemen wearing gypsy gear somewhat cheered the young men. And, after all, what had they to lose by taking a chance? To go back to Scotland with empty hands would be intolerable.

Ian describes how he and Bill walked slowly down across the field. 'In the leaping flames we could see an ancient gypsy couple sprawled against the fence, their boots outstretched to the blaze. The man could have put his hand through the fence and touched the Stone.' Bill asked if they could have a heat at the fire. Welcomed in, he sat for a long time without saying anything. A supremely talented communicator, eventually Bill began to generalise about the cold. Gently, with many pauses, he steered the conversation round to the situation of Travellers, how they were constantly harried, about the need for rights and freedom, and to the Scottish people in the north who, like the gypsies, were trying to retain their ways and their freedoms and how, in order to achieve certain aims in that direction, he urgently needed something that was behind the caravan.

In the end, two of the gypsies courteously helped carry the Stone to the car, where it was placed in lieu of the passenger seat and covered with a travelling rug. Ian still feels 'despicable' when he remembers how he mistakenly offered money in thanks. It was politely refused. The whole incident retains for him an element of the supernatural: 'Sometimes I wonder if they were really there, yet they must have been, for we all saw and spoke to them. But why? Out of all the broad acres and highways and lanes of England, why on that exact spot? Within one yard? Why on that exact night of all nights?' For nothing could more effectively have hidden the Stone.

Taking turns at sitting on the Stone, they drove north up the A6. At York Johnny was reluctantly dropped at the station with the real passenger seat, to continue his journey by train. A Yorkshire petrol pump operator said cheerily that the police had been there earlier asking what Scotsmen he'd sold petrol to. Ian managed to hold his nerve long enough to make a crack about the Stone being in the boot. Exhaustion and nervous tension, as the border approached, were beginning to affect him.

At half past two that Hogmanay they drove the Stone of Scone across the border and into Scotland. Hamilton writes:

'Success is a strange thing, much nearer to tears than to laughter.' A few miles further on they stopped, to expose the Stone to Scottish air, to pour a libation of whisky over it, and drink a toast: to the Stone, to each other, and to the new Scotland they were going to build.

Later that evening they arrived in Glasgow. The whole adventure had cost a total of seventy pounds. All those involved now faced arrest, prosecution and imprisonment. And they had no idea whatsoever what to do with their cargo. Ian phoned Bertie Gray, and while they waited for him outside the King's Theatre in Glasgow, found himself munching a fish supper, sitting on the Stone in the car. He says, 'I had never been in a more bizarre situation.'

Gray arrived and said: 'Drive out towards Stirling. I've got the very man.'

Others were destined to whisk the Stone into hiding. Ian's task was at an end. The Stone of Scone was back in Scotland. Did anybody know? Did anybody care? And did Hamilton and his confederates succeed in their aim of arousing the Scottish people in any way?

CHAPTER TWO

≈

THE HOSTAGE STONE

John Rollo, lunching in his works canteen on Christmas Day 1950, was blissfully unaware of the part he was about to play. He knew nothing of the plot to take the Stone until he heard what had happened on the one-o'clock radio news. He was highly amused.

Rollo was a benevolent industrialist who believed Scotland needed local employment. When Kay Matheson's mother offered the ex-army site on her croft for one of his factories, he accepted. 'It was going until he died,' said Kay, 'which meant that there was four young families who didn't have to go away from the district, and one old man. It made a big difference in Inverasdale. He was a dedicated man. It's a pity there weren't more like him. There are Nationalists who are genuine, but not down to earth in a practical way like him.'

Singer and broadcaster Jimmie MacGregor remembers 'the ripple of delight that ran through Scotland when we heard that the Stone had returned. It was a great joke, and we admired the sheer nose-thumbing cheek of the venture. We were aware that another buttress had been erected against the crumbling fabric of our identity'. He and partner Robin Hall began to sing Johnny McEvoy's composition '*The Wee Magic Stane*'.

Because nobody had any idea where the Stone was, or what sort of people had taken it, rumours were whizzing about. Had our ancient and most venerated relic been hidden safely? Was a bunch of silly students taking risks with it? Could cranks simply have disposed of it? Concern was expressed in the newspapers and on radio, and apparently King George VI himself was anxious about its safety, realising the affair could have far-reaching consequences.

The worldwide press published articles and letters, with varying degrees of accuracy, as journalists broke legs in the race for scoops. 'Stone still missing – wrist-watch found – people who took it are cranks – Block of concrete dredged up from Serpentine – Petition to the King left at a Glasgow newspaper office . . .'

Two days after the disappearance of the Stone, Dr A.C. Don, the Scottish Dean of Westminster, addressed the nation. He spoke of his feelings when the Clerk of Works had rushed into his bedroom and told him that the Coronation Stone had gone. Never, until this week, had anyone dared to lay sacrilegious hands on this precious relic which was treasured by millions, and the King had let him know that he was greatly distressed. Listeners were told to keep their eyes and ears open – and that Dr Don would 'go to the ends of the earth to fetch it back'. Dr Don promptly left London 'for three days rest', said the papers, emphasising that 'the Dean had *not* gone to Scotland'.

His agitation was understandable. King George knew privately that he had only a few months to live, and wanted to be sure that his daughter would be properly crowned on the Stone. People had a real affection for the King, quite different from the mixture of speculation, adulation and ridicule showered on royalty today.

Public apologies began to pour southward. The SNP, attempting to gain respectability, wrote to King George deploring the way 'ill-disposed persons' were embroiling him in a controversy about national property 'unlawfully acquired' and saying that the 'theft' had revived racialist tendencies.

While Glasgow University creaked its ancient bones into celebrating five centuries of existence, legal and political questions were aired: the Stone belonged neither to King nor Church but to the Scottish people. If the Scots people had proper constitutional means of expressing their will. . . Was this felony or larceny, or hooliganism? The American magazine *Time* devoted a whole page to the Stone.

Scots did begin to worry about what the neighbours thought. The act was perpetuating superstition, bringing ridicule on Scotland's 'Stone Age' mentality. John Cameron KC, a prominent Covenant leader, and Dr Neville Davidson, Minister of Glasgow Cathedral, pleaded for the return of the Stone to Westminster. Scots should seek legal means to have its custody in Scotland, if their reform requirements were to be taken seriously. Dr Henry Meikle, Historiographer Royal for Scotland, made notes on the Stone's history.

Meanwhile, Scotland Yard was still busy hunting for clues. After the wrist-watch, someone found a plaque about the Stone on a bombsite five hundred yards from the Abbey. There were those who blamed the English for what had happened. England's refusal to restore the Stone to Scotland, as a civilised neighbour, had resulted in the loss of this Scottish national relic.

A meeting was held in St Andrew's Hall, Glasgow, at which the perpetrators of 'the glorious deed' were cheered. Dr Mary Ramsay challenged the audience: 'If the men of Scotland cannot find a way to get it [the Stone], then the women of Scotland certainly will', to applause.

Sensible folk earned a bob or two selling plaster models of the coronation chair and Stone to London's tourists. Wendy Wood wrote energetically about how the retrieving of the Stone had produced national panic in England, and a rejuvenation of national consciousness in Scotland. England, she said,

> wailed like a war siren . . . forgetting . . . that one of their most honourable kings, Richard Coeur de Lion, had signed a document for its return to Scotland, but the merchants of London would not let it go . . . A reward of £2,000 was offered to informers, but had no more effect than a former offer of £30,000 for the person of Prince Charles Edward. . . Everyone hoped that his next door neighbour had it.

Being a known Nationalist, Wendy Wood was the recipient of correspondence from a variety of bodies. *Brith*, the journal of the British Israelites, threatened that unless the Stone was returned at once to 'the King of Israel, George VI', all connected with the theft would be cursed. Her response was that 'God could be relied on to size up the situation in Scotland's favour.' The then Earl of Thomond in Ireland wrote to her too. Claiming descent from Brian Boru, King of Ireland, and, as such, the rightful owner of the Irish Stone, the *Lia Fail*, he named her Guardian of the Stone.

Wendy Wood was, of course, a suspect. In March, knowing the CID were after her, she stocked up her Moidart croft house and went to Glasgow, hoping they would follow her and thus leave the croft as a safe haven for any fugitive Stone carriers. She told MacCormick about a good underwater mooring where the Stone could be hidden in her loch.

Long after the events of 1951, John Rollo made a secret recording in which he agreed to tell the truth about what happened after that Hogmanay of 1950, provided it would not be released till after his death. Since then the BBC has broadcast it on several occasions. In his clipped, matter-of-fact Scots voice Rollo tells how, at half past six on 31st December, he was busy stock-taking in his Bonnybridge works. The phone rang. It was Bertie Gray asking how long he would be at the works – two people wanted to see him. Rollo promised to wait.

When they arrived, Gray told him the Coronation Stone was in the car and asked would Rollo, as a good Scot, look after it for a time? Rollo agreed, and ran out with him to the Armstrong Siddeley. The Stone under its rug was still acting as the front seat. After cooking the young drivers a hearty meal, Rollo found himself left alone with the Stone.

Next morning – New Year's Day – Rollo returned to the empty factory, built a strong packing case and, using overhead gear, lifted the Stone into it. Removing the planking from a space beneath his foreman's office, he manoeuvered the case into it and sealed it with nails which he instantly rusted, using sal-ammoniac.

The press were soon on his tail, as his sympathies were known. On about the 12th January David Forrester, Secretary of the Covenant committee, phoned him late at night. Would he come over, urgently?

Rollo skidded through eight-inch-deep snow to Bishop-briggs, where Alan Stuart's father offered him an H.P. Sauce carton, containing Kay's portion of the Stone. He drove it back to his factory and stuck it in the kneehole of his desk.

The police kept an eye on all known nationalists. Before long, a bright young Detective Inspector, William Kerr, had an idea. He knew of the earlier plot, and took into custody the fake stone made twenty years before. It had been written about. He went to the Mitchell Library – and discovered the names and addresses of three students on application slips: Ian Hamilton, Gavin Vernon and Alan Stuart. Interviewed, none of them now had any idea where the evidence was. The police haunted Rollo's factories around the Highlands, one of which had been built on the Matheson croft at Inverasdale, asking if anyone had recently noticed any unusually heavy packing cases.

'A detective was sent from Glasgow,' says Kay Matheson, 'Calum Robertson – he had Gaelic. He thought nobody knew who he was, and he went and stayed with his relations at Sheildaig Lodge Hotel, who immediately phoned me to say it was him. All the folk knew that he was a Skye man, and what he was there for. And the yarns they were telling him! They had him away up at a loch in the hill, and he was buying them drams – they had the night of their lives – what a fool they made of him. His pocket was empty by the time he went off – and all for nothing.

'Another lot came questioning me, and I said – well, if they wouldn't tell anyone, it was in the peat bank. I had all my peats cut! All the old bodachs, the old men, were saying "you could have told us first and we'd have told them it was in our peat". The old folk had a right good laugh.'

Meanwhile, Rollo rented storage space for several large boxes of unspecified heavy goods, from his old friend Tommy Smith, who ran David Goodfellow & Co near Stirling. With some difficulty he transported the heavy crate to Goodfellow's. His co-director, James Scott, put the H.P. Sauce carton in his garage.

Rollo let it be known that Bertie Gray was keeping one or more than one accurate reproduction of the Coronation Stone in his monumental yard. Scotland Yard, thrashing about in a frenzy of frustrated detection, noted that Cromwell's bust had been knocked sideways. Could this be a clue? Eventually they were driven to employ a Dutch clairvoyant, who announced that he saw the Stone lying in an old building alongside a river, beside a bridge, near an ancient church. The river ran through a capital city. Of course Scotland Yard could only think of one capital city: London. The Thames was searched as far upriver as Reading.

Goodfellows' factory – an old building – was on the Stirling side of the footbridge over to Cambuskenneth Abbey, alongside the Forth – which runs through Edinburgh. The clairvoyant had been astoundingly accurate.

Towards the end of March, MacCormick and Gray asked Rollo to hand over the Stone. He was reluctant to give it back until he knew and approved of what was going to happen to it. But he had a special mason's handbarrow made by Stuart Henderson, a Perth coachbuilder. In Glasgow, after a dummy run with a bag of coal during which he was nearly caught by the police, he finally managed to deliver the Stone to the house of Willie White in respectable Bearsden. MacCormick and Gray were there with a mason. It was the evening of Easter Monday 1951. Rollo watched as the mason began to chisel holes for two brass dowels which would help to hold the repaired Stone together and knew his role as caretaker was over.

William Kerr, in charge of Glasgow City Special Branch, headed the hunt for the Stone. In a private statement to the Scottish Office, he said that 'only by the narrowest margin' had they failed to track it down before it reappeared on 11th April. To the press he said, 'The students who took the Stone were a clever bunch – they have all since made their mark professionally.' He himself ended up as Chief Constable of Dumbartonshire. His dossier lay in a black Government briefcase belonging to the then permanent Under-Secretary of state at the Scottish Office – Sir William Kerr Fraser, more recently Principal of Glasgow University. When Sir William retired, it was deposited in the University archive.

The next thing Rollo saw was a newspaper picture of Arbroath Abbey, and a familiar-looking sandstone block draped in the Scottish flag. His voice was full of disgust as he told of the shameful way the Stone was abandoned at the High Altar, and of how the people in charge of it skulked away.

William Bishop, Scots-born clerk of works at Westminster Abbey, was despatched to Arbroath to identify the Stone before it was taken back.

Wendy Wood takes up the tale. It was 13th April 1951. She was walking along a street in Dumbarton when a bus conductor shouted to her that the Stone was now in Forfar Police station. She rushed to Glasgow, collected fifteen students, threw them on to a train to Forfar – where they missed the removal of the Stone by twenty minutes, as it sped to Glasgow Central Police Station. 'The English did not dare to prosecute the raiders,' she writes, 'even when at last they knew who they were.'

Then the rumours started up again. Was it the same Stone that had been brought from Westminster? If not, who had it? In the mid-1960s a mysterious Stone turned up in Parliament Square, Edinburgh. The Revd John Mackay Nimmo, a staunch Nationalist, Minister of St Columba's Church in Dundee, Chaplain to the Knights of St John, recalls that he was asked if he would be prepared to take this Stone into Sanctuary.

> We had a service attended by Nationalists from all over Scotland and we accepted the Stone. Baillie Gray was at this service and there he assured me that this was the real Stone of Destiny. It was well known in the town,

one of the landmarks of the place. The very night the Stone came here the Chief Constable of Dundee said he'd heard that I had stolen property in my church. 'Well,' I said, 'this is true. But it is a question of who has stolen it.' In the morning he said 'I've been in touch with the authorities' – I presume he meant at Westminster – 'and they said that they had their Stone and they were happy with it.' We had our Stone and he was happy about that.

Dr Hugh Ryan, one of the Stone's historians, firmly believed that the one in Westminster Abbey was genuine. With a laugh and a sniff, so you don't know if he's serious, he talked on another old recording about his friend Bertie Gray, saying how he wouldn't trust him, that his stories were doubtful. He even told the police not to believe Gray because of his mischievous Scots sense of humour and his fondness for deliberately creating mysteries.

But questions about the provenance of the Stone went on. Amateur Historian Archie McKerracher, who wrote about the Stone in the 1980s, said 'Bertie Gray made two copies; one in 1928 and one in 1950. I think that the 1950 copy is now the stone in Westminster Abbey beneath the coronation chair. The 1928 copy which wasn't quite as accurate is in the church in Dundee, and the Westminster Stone is at a secret location in the Arbroath area . . . it is produced on certain occasions and taken through the streets of Arbroath. I don't think the Westminster people, having got *a* stone back, were going to quibble.'

Gray, before sealing the join in the Stone, dug out a little space and filled it with a piece of paper on which he had written 'This Stone was stolen by Edward I in 1296 and it should be returned to Scotland'. The crumbs he divided between those involved in the taking.

Ten years later Gray was saying in a newspaper interview, 'Oh I can't really be sure which Stone I sent back to London – there were so many copies lying about.' Ryan said quizzically that, while Gray loved a chance to take the mickey out of the credulous English, he later told Nimmo that he was giving *him* the real Stone. Frank J. Dimes of London, Chief Scientific Officer of the Institute of Geological Sciences, tried to identify the returned stone through minute inspection. He found that it did contain pea-sized volcanic pebbles, not unlike those he had noted in the original, and there was no doubt now that the Stone had been quarried in eastern Perthshire not far from Scone. Of course any sculptor worth his sporran would have gone to Perthshire for raw materials for his spoof rock – there's plenty left where the Stone of Scone came from, containing matching volcanic pebbles. In 1975 Gray went to his grave, his secret intact, at the age of seventy-nine.

Ian Hamilton believes that Westminster received the real Stone of Scone. Rollo's daughter, Margaret, maintains that the stone her father looked after is the one that went back to Westminster. But Kay Matheson, who is in no doubt about her view ('I most definitely didn't think it should be given back to England') says of the Westminster authorities: 'Well – if it's the real Stone they got back . . .' and her voice tails off, her eyes twinkling with mischief.

Wendy Wood wrote, 'It was a piece of sophistry that still makes one blink . . . The Stone, we were told, was no use hidden. It could not much longer remain undetected, and it was better to give it up than have it taken.' Some thought that if the authorities dared to snatch the Stone back to England, they would outrage Scottish feeling, motivating them sufficiently to push for change.

Wood was not yet done with the Stone. In 1968 she

went to the Abbey and slipped a piece of cardboard under the complicated iron railings (as high as a deer fence) on which was printed, '*This is not the original Stone of Destiny. The real Stone is of black basalt marked with hieroglyphics and is inside a hill in Scotland*'. I stood and enjoyed . . . the grovellings of the officials as they tried to get any part of their anatomy under their own wrought iron restrictions. As there is a lens in the middle of a Tudor rose in the chapel opposite, which automatically registers anything that passes the railing, I wondered what comic cuts were perhaps being produced.

A brief diary of what happened to the returned Stone is noted in the Westminster copy of Hamilton's book, ending 'Kept in vault, replaced in Chair 26th Feb 1952'.

From papers released on 17th July 1996, it seems clear that Clement Attlee was on the brink of returning the Stone when Churchill and his Conservatives won the election. Six volumes of classified Government documents were opened to scrutiny in a small reading room of the General Registrar's office in Edinburgh, revealing how civil servants were told to search for a suitable home for it. Six options were considered in a Scottish Office briefing: Dunstaffnage, Iona and Scone for their connections with the Stone; St Giles Cathedral in Edinburgh, and Stirling Castle, the preferred place being St Margaret's Chapel at Edinburgh Castle. Attlee wanted to send it on a tour of Commonwealth capitals. But the new Conservative Secretary of State for Scotland decided the Stone belonged in Westminster Abbey. On 16th August the Prime Minister's Office informed the Scottish Office that Don, the Dean, wanted the Stone back on display. King George VI died in February 1952 and the Stone reappeared in the Abbey shortly after his funeral. Winston Churchill eventually informed the public, after much discussion of the actual words chosen, that it had been returned to 'its traditional place' which, he later told the Commons, 'commanded wide acceptance on both sides of the Border'.

And there, it would seem, the story of the Coronation Stone ends. Or does it?

CHAPTER THREE

≈

QUEENS, KINGS AND
CORONATION CHAIRS

The Coronation Stone may now be kept in Scotland, but as soon as the next monarch needs to be crowned, the Westminster authorities are to whisk it south again for the ceremony. Why do both Scots and English care so much that our monarchs should be sat on a dusty old piece of sandstone as part of their inauguration, so much that they've been arguing about it for seven hundred years?

King-making ceremonies have been evolving for thousands of years. In Egypt, the pharaohs wore crowns to symbolise their royal rank. In ancient Greece and Rome, athletes and poets were crowned with laurel wreaths, in recognition of their public service. David was crowned and anointed King of Israel and the early Church, believing him to be the forefather of all kings, did its best to emulate his ceremony for subsequent coronations. Since the fourteenth century the Catholic Church itself has bestowed the tiara – a triple crown – upon its popes.

In England, each coronation requires the public consent of the populace, and the sovereign must swear an oath that she will govern according to certain requirements. There is consecration by the Church through prayer, anointment with holy oil, investiture with the regalia (which symbolically clothe the monarch in the office of sovereignty), enthronement in the seat of government, and communion to seal the pact with God.

Scottish monarchs, however, came to power on a quite different set of principles. Professor Archie Duncan tells how stone has been used for this since the earliest times: 'It is undoubtedly an ancient ritual, seating a ruler down as the symbol of inauguration.'

This practice is first recorded in AD 800, with Charlemagne, whose *Marmorne Stuhl* or marble chair can still be seen at Aix-la-Chapelle in France. It is a plain, heavy seat of white marble mounted on five steps. At coronations it was covered with gold. Stone was also used in Ireland, where the new king would place his foot in the footprint of his predecessor as he took the various oaths. This footprint was most usually gouged out of 'living' rock – that is, outcrop rock which is part of the underlying geological structure. Occasionally footprints are also found on movable boulders. Could it be that these ancient people thought the basic elements of life on the planet – sun, water and stone – made reliable witnesses to promises and vows? Certainly stone has been used as a witness to human activity since the earliest times, from Jacob in the book of Genesis to the standing stones we see in northern Europe, and to beautiful Pictish carvings like those which cover the entire surface of Sueno's Stone, by the Moray Firth. We still bear witness to the lives of our loved ones by placing a headstone above their graves.

'Why would they think up a Stone?' asks Professor Ted Cowan. 'Because they definitely did inaugurate their kings on stone. No question.'

Professor Duncan doubts the Scottish stone was ever actually a ritual object in itself. He says the point was the *sitting* of the person, and that the use of stone goes back for hundreds of years before we hear of it and possibly even for a thousand or more. It was an ancient symbol of the king's marriage to the people, 'whom he swore to rule in justice, and perhaps once, long before Columba's day, a symbol of the king's marriage to the goddess who brought fertility to his land.' The stone was used 'perhaps to represent the territory of the people'. If it is taken as Jacob's Pillow, it again carries that idea; 'the land whereon thou liest, to thee will I give it, and to thy seed' as God said. Professor Duncan says, 'despite what Edward I removed in 1296, it was probaby used again when Robert the Bruce was enthroned as king in 1306, a hurried ceremony indeed, but one carefully prepared to replicate the ceremonies of the ancient line of kings from whom he claimed to inherit.' We read that Bruce sat on 'the kingis stole [stool].' Enthronement was the secular act of king-making, and was practised at Kingston on Thames in Anglo-Saxon times and in Westminster from 1066 to 1954.

Thanks to their appropriation of the Stone of Scone at the end of the thirteenth century, the English added Scottish notions of inauguration to their ceremony. For a time the anointing, investiture and crowning of the sovereign were private ceremonies, carried out by the lords spiritual, and taking place on the coronation chair in the sanctuary of the abbey. Monarchs were required to strip to the waist for the anointing, and then had to 'grovel' before the High Altar.

For the public, secular part of the ceremony, carried out by the lords temporal, a throne was set on a stage beneath the crossing so that all present could see their monarch. From this throne the newly crowned sovereign received homage from the people.

In the present century British coronations have become more elaborate. The ceremony now consists of four sections: *The introduction*, when the Archbishop of Canterbury ushers in the sovereign and presents her to the assembled throng, extracting from her a promise to govern according to law. *The anointing* is done on the coronation chair, under a canopy held by four Knights of the Garter. Holy oil is poured into a spoon through the beak of a gold eagle. The archbishop anoints the sovereign's head, hands and breast while the choir sings 'Zadok the Priest'. Zadok was priest to King David of Israel, and to the young King Solomon, from whom all monarchs including the English ones are supposed to descend and through whom they once claimed their Divine Right to govern. *The investiture* involves the sovereign being dressed in white linen and cloth of gold, and given spurs, a sword, an orb, a ring, the sceptre symbolising power and justice, and a rod with a dove on it symbolising equity and mercy. Finally, the archbishop places the crown on her head. While the present crown is not very old, it is said to contain the original crown of Edward the Confessor (r. 1042–66), who was a contemporary of the Scottish king, Macbeth. *The Enthronement* comes only after the people acclaim their new sovereign by expressing their approval in loud cheers before they pay homage to her.

Professor Duncan reminds us that the usurper Henry IV was the first king to be crowned in the coronation chair, in 1399. The *Westminster Abbey Official Guide* confesses that Edward I had ordered the chair 'to enclose the famous Stone of Scone, which he seized in 1296 and brought from Scotland to the Abbey'. This Stone weighed 990 kilos (four hundredweight), and Edward I had iron rings fixed to each side for its journey south. Since then it has been used by every monarch. Even Oliver Cromwell thought its magic might be helpful, and used it for his installation as Lord Protector.

In Scotland, inaugurations of early *Ardrigh*, provincial kings, were simple affairs by comparison. Picture the scene: an area such as Dalriada (Argyll) not long after the Romans had left Britain; close to the *Ardrigh*, with his right foot planted in the excised footprint on the stone of honour at the summit of Dunadd Hill, stands the *Righdomna* or *Tanist*, the heir-apparent to the monarchy, who has been nominated according to the fundamental Celtic principle of shared authority. Although by the ninth century Pictish kingship was patrilinear, there are those who believe it was once elective, and that from this stemmed the practice which pervaded all the institutions of the Gaelic people, who chose their clan chiefs, their *Ardrigh*, in this way.

'We do know that we've got these inauguration footprint stones,' says Professor Cowan. 'But that seems to be incompatible with the idea of a movable stone. At Scone what's shown on the seals is a wee seat.'

When Scots reached the stage of having a single king, around the ninth century, it's thought that he was inaugurated by sitting on a bare stone in the open air. As the centuries wore on the stone was draped with silk, dressing it up more and more till eventually, by the thirteenth century, as we can see from the old royal seals, it was enshrined in elaborately carved wood. Where else could Edward I have got the idea for the coronation chair he ordered so quickly?

Professor Cowan is 'not absolutely convinced that the tantalising references we get earlier to inauguration stones are actually references to the one at Scone. We don't know *where* our kings were inaugurated – it's not stated. In Ireland there were inaugurations on stone at one point, then it goes out, then they consciously bring it back in again in the thirteenth century as a statement of Irish sovereignty vis-a-vis the English. I think it's very likely that something similar happened in Scotland.'

The first documented Scottish inauguration is that of Alexander III, in 1249, described by an Aberdeen Chantry Priest, John of Fordoun, thus:

> Alexander . . . a boy of eight years old, came to Scone . . . on . . . Tuesday, the 13th of July. There were present the venerable fathers David de Bernham, Bishop of St Andrews, and Galfridus, Bishop of Dunkeld . . . [and] the Abbott of the same monastery of Scone . . . [They] led the future King Alexander to the cross, which stands in the *cimiterium* or churchyard at the east end of the church; and, having there placed him in the regal chair, decked with silk cloths embroidered with gold, the Bishop of St Andrews, the others assisting him, consecrated him king, the king himself sitting, as was proper, upon the regal chair – that is, the Stone – and the earls and other nobles placing vestments under his feet, with bent knees, before the Stone.
>
> This Stone is reverently preserved in that monastery for the consecration of kings of Scotland; nor were any of the kings in wont to reign anywhere in Scotland, unless they had, on receiving the name of the king, first sat upon this royal Stone in Scone, which was constituted by ancient kings the *sedes superior* or principal seat, that is to say, of Albania [Alba].

Two features of the English ceremony are absent from this inauguration: anointing and crowning.

Professor Cowan explains: 'The Scots definitely felt inferior because they did not have unction – anoinment – when the king is crowned. They'd applied to the pope for unction several times, apparently, and they'd always been blocked by the English. Because, if the Scots got unction, then Scotland would have to be recognised as an independent nation. Some guys went off to the coronation of Magnus of Norway. They were quite stunned when they saw his spectacular ceremony, and knew that this did not happen with their own kings.'

The point about crowning and anointing was that they were Christian symbols which showed the king was inaugurated by God's grace.

It took an English king, agrees Professor Duncan, to subvert the independence of his neighbouring country. Edward I did his best to convince the pope that Scottish kings were not sovereign rulers because they were not crowned and anointed. Previous kings had tried to secure the right to these ceremonies, but were always denied 'because opposed at Rome by the English'. Five Christian lands with such rights grew to ten and more, 'but Scotland was still excluded'.

Although in 1278 Alexander III informed Edward I that he held his kingdom 'of God alone and not of any earthly ruler', no Scottish king was both crowned and anointed until David II, who succeeded his father Robert I in June 1329, and celebrated his coronation in November 1331, thanks to Robert the Bruce's successful attempt at persuading the pope to recognise Scotland as a nation in its own right at last, separate from England.

But in order to do this, it seems he had to engage the services of a rather creative historian. Could it be that the tale of the Stone of Destiny only ever emanated from a story-teller whose sole aim was to boost Scotland's credit in Europe?

≈

CHAPTER FOUR

HOW THE LEGENDS BEGAN

Baldred Bisset is blamed for obfuscating Scottish history, recycling legends and creating new myths. Professor Cowan does see 'an element of manufacture about this. The agenda is part of the polemic that's flying about between the Scots and the English. This may be why we have such a detailed account of the inauguration of Alex III and information about John Baliol. That Baliol affair is very quickly followed by the Baldred Bisset account about the Stone, because Edward's taken away the Stone, he's taken away the Black Rood. Bisset's saying this is significant, but he also wants to show what a bastard Edward is – he'd no right to do such a thing. I don't see much *evidence* of legends, for instance about Scota and so on, before the end of the thirteenth century.'

For some, legend and myth will always mean fairytales, even lies, but for others they represent the efforts made by human beings to make sense of things that once actually happened. Increasingly, historians and anthropologists are finding useful sources of information in these traditional stories, and sometimes vital clues, which can start archaeologists on trails that lead to the discovery of fascinating pieces of the jigsaw that makes up our past. Every few years evidence turns up which corroborates some ancient myth. New methods of detection continue to be invented, such as geophysics, where satellites are used to discover what is hidden underground, while ancient skills like dowsing are still usefully employed. It may be that all the clues we need to find the Stone are there for the taking – if only we could recognise them.

For hundreds of years the stories about the Stone of Destiny remained flexibly in the oral tradition of Scotland, flourishing in a compost of memories, misunderstandings and wishful thinking. In order for folklore to endure, however, it must be animated with the spirit of truth and reason, and it must contain, from whatever distance of time, and however difficult to recognise, a nugget of fact. Otherwise it simply withers and dies with its own generation. Storyteller Duncan Williamson was born into culture in which you learned not by reading and writing but by listening, observing and remembering. Aged fifteen he took to the road himself, and has been in the best possible position to understand the organic quality of story, and how it mutates according to its audience. In the absence of written records, Scots owe an enormous debt to people like Williamson and the ballad-singers, and to those who collect their lore, such as Dr Hamish Henderson of the School of Scottish Studies in Edinburgh.

History gives us the fact that the British people have long regarded the Stone of Destiny as some kind of talisman. Folklore tells us how and why they do so: for its magical and protective powers over the Scots. Modern journalism explores the reasons why the Westminster authorities hung on to the Stone for seven centuries, in spite of the many treaties England has made promising its return.

The legend comes down to us in spoken and in written form and some of the early writers used written sources that have since disappeared. Each of the accounts varies in detail, and spellings change too, but parts of the story and many names remain consistent. Only by working through their complexities can we see how the story grew.

The Victorians took an interest in the Stone. In 1866 Joseph Robertson of Register House, Edinburgh, enumerated a few facts he had gleaned from Scottish chronicles, written at various periods from the tenth century, which showed that at least as early as 906 Scone was a royal city, the meeting place of a national council or assembly, and Scottish kings were crowned there *super Cathedram Regadem lapideam* (on a royal stone chair). The oldest writer who tells the legend of the Royal Stone is William of Rishanger, an English annalist who lived until after 1327, and who describes the coronation in 1292 of king John Balliol at Scone, *super lapidem Regadem* (on a royal stone). Robertson also cites Andrew of Wyntoun, a prior of St Serf's in Loch Leven, who wrote a *Metrical Chronicle of Scotland* about 1424, in which Simon Brek's father, the king of Spain, gave him 'a gret Stane that for thei Kyngis sete was made' and bade him take it to Ireland:

> And wyn that land and occupy,
> And halde that Stane perpetually,
> And make it his sege Stane
> As thai of Spayne did of it ane.

Robertson also argued that there must have been two Stones at Scone, believing that while Edward I took 'the Stone of Fate' to Westminster, there remained at Scone 'a Stone Chair, in which it would seem the Stone of Fate was placed when kings were to be inaugurated . . . in 1306 we read that king Robert Bruce was placed in the Royal Seat at Scone. So also king Robert II . . . we have record of his sitting next day in the Royal Seat on the Moothill of Scone.'

The earliest written version of the Stone of Destiny legend discovered in recent times is quoted by English folklorist Jennifer Westwood in her book *Albion* (1985). It comes from a monk, Robert of Gloucester (1230–1300), who traces the first Irish immigrations. He says they

> broghte into Scotland a whyte marble ston,
> Zat was ordeyned for hure kyng, whan he coroned wer.
> And for a grete Jewyll long hit was yholde ther.

Westwood suggests that Edward I took it to England 'because he was a superstitious man who fully believed in the power of the *Fatale Marmor* . . . the Stone of Fate. For the stone was invested with mana . . . it very likely *did* come from Ireland with the Scots'. She reminds us that the custom of using stone 'had to do with the cult of the ancestor, whose spirits perhaps dwelt in the stone, so that the newly invested king received the "luck" or mana of his predecessors by contact with it'. In Norway kings were enthroned on the burial mounds of their forebears, probably for similar reasons.

The Victorian Professor William Skene examined the documentary evidence:

> Hector Boece wrote the *Scotorum Historiae* in 1537, in which Gaythelus, a Greek, the son either of the Athenian Cecrops or the Argive Neolus, went to Egypt at the time of the Exodus, where he married Scota, the daughter of Pharao, and after the destruction of the Egyptian army in the Red Sea, fled with her by the Mediterranenan till he arrived in Portingall, where he landed, and founded a kingdom at Brigantium, now Compostella. Here he reigned in the marbile chair, which was the '*lapis fatalis cathedrae instar*', or fatal stone like a chair, and wherever it was found portended kingdom to the Scots . . . Simon Breck, a descendant of Gathelus, brought the chair from Spain to Ireland, and was crowned in it as King of Ireland . . . Fergus, son of Ferchard, was first King of the Scots in Scotland, and brought the chair from Ireland to Argyll, and was crowned in it. He built a town in Argyll called Beregonium, in which he placed it . . . The twelfth king, Evenus, built a town near Beregonium, called after his name Evonium, now called Dunstaffnage, to which the stone was removed . . .

Eventually Fergus Mac Erc 'is crowned in the marble chair. He builds a church at Iona, and commands it to be the sepulchre of the kings in future.'

The *Scalacronica*, compiled in 1355, begins with Simon Brec, youngest son of the King of Spain, bringing to Ireland 'a stone on which the kings of Spain were wont to be crowned'. Brec 'placed it in the most sovereign beautiful place in Ireland, called to this day the Royal Place (Tara), and Fergus, son of Ferchar, brought the royal stone before received, and placed it where is now the Abbey of Scone'. Here the Stone moves directly from Ireland to Scone.

The earliest history of Scotland, the *Scotichronicon*, by Fordun, who was alive in 1386, is a little thinner. He says Gaythelus married a Pharaoh's daughter – Scota – and led those who weren't drowned in the Red Sea through Africa to Spain. A Spanish king descended from him sent his son, Simon Brec, to Ireland, presenting him with 'the *Marmorea Cathedra*, the marble chair, diligently and carefully sculptured by ancient art, on which the kings of Spain, of Scottish race were wont to sit'. This stone chair he placed in Tara, 'the royal seat and principal place of the kingdom of Ireland'. Fordun quotes the *Ni fallat fatum* prophecy and says that Fergus, who led the Scots from Ireland to Scotland, brought with him 'the royal chair cut out of marble stone, in which he was crowned first king there by the Scots, after whose example the succeeding kings received the rite of coronation in the same chair'.

Skene sums up the 'facts' he has gleaned from these pieces of evidence; 'It is true that such a stone was preserved at Scone; it is true that Scottish monarchs were crowned upon it; and it is true that in 1296 Edward I removed it to Westminster Abbey, where it now is, and can be seen under the seat of the Coronation Chair.' Nowadays we may have reservations as to the accuracy of some of these 'truths'.

When Fordun, who died less than a hundred years after Alexander III, wrote that the young king sat 'as was proper, upon the regal chair – that is, the stone,' the folk-memory was still fresh. It is known that Fordun collected some of his information from sources now lost to us and we can feel reasonably happy that his account was accurate: there was indeed a special stone used in the king-making ceremony at Scone. Rishanger had written in his *Chronica et Annales* (1327), 'John de Balioll. . . (*collocatus super lapidem regadem*) – placed upon the regal stone – which Jacob placed under his head when he went from Bersabee to Haran, was solemnly crowned . . . at Scone'. As an Englishman, Rishanger had no particular reason to lie, so again we can probably take it as a fact that the Stone was still in use in 1292 at Balliol's inauguration. But when Rishanger goes on to say that Edward I 'passed by the Abbey of Scone, where having taken away *the* stone which the Kings of Scotland were wont at the time of their coronation to use for a throne, carried it to Westminster' (the original Latin reads: '*ubi sublato lapide quo Reges Scotorum, tempore coronationis, solebant uti pro throno, usque Westmonasterium transtulit illum, jubens inde fieri celebrantium cathedram sacerdotum*') many historians now harbour doubts, for reasons which may become apparent.

The second-earliest written source of information comes in the form of two extant manuscripts of what at first appears to be a poem, written after the death of Edward I in 1307, entitled 'La Piere D'Escoce'.

> *Qei est la piere de Escose, vous die pur verite,*
> *Sur qei les Roys d'Escoce estoint mis en see.*
> *Johan Balol le drein fust, a ceo q'est counte,*
> *Qe sur ceste piere resceut sa dignite.*
>
> *Ore l'ad conquise Edward Roy d'Engleterre,*
> *Par la grace Jhesu Criste et par forte guere.*
> *A Seint Edward la present com roy de graunt affaire.*
> *Ore est passe par la morte que nul ne poet retrere.*
>
> *En Egipte Moise a le poeple precha,*
> *Scota la file Faraun bien l'escola,*
> *Qare il dite en espirite, 'Qe ceste piere avera,*
> *De molt estraunge terre conquerour serra.*
>
> *Gaidelons et Scota cest piere menerount*
> *Quant de la terre Egipte en Escose passerount,*
> *Ne geres loyns de Scone quant ariveront.*
> *De la noun de Scota la Escose terre numount.*
>
> *Puis la mort la Scota son baron femme ne prist,*
> *Mais en la terre de Galway sa demore fist.*
> *De son noune demoisne le noune de Galway mist.*
> *Issi pert qe pare lour nouns Escose et Galway ist.*
>
> *Ore est Edward passe hors de ceste vie,*
> *Conquerour de terres, la flour de chivalrie,*
> *Prioms Dieu omnipotent, qe tout le mounde guye,*
> *Qe Dieu de s'alme eyt mercy, Dieu le fitz Marye.*

The late Dominica Legge, Reader in French at Edinburgh University, made a detailed study of this work, demonstrating that it had probably once been a song. The irrelevant detail that Gaidelon remained a widower after Scota's death suggests that the original source for 'La Piere D'Escoce' was much fuller. The style in which the poem is set out was rare after the twelfth century in England, and so may well be the cut-down version of a much older lyric. Legge reminds us that this version of Moses' prophecy is corroborated in another fourteenth century English manuscript, the *Vita Edwardi II*.

She translates the work thus;

> What the Stone of Scotland is, I tell you for truth, on which the Kings of Scotland were placed in their seat. John Baliol was the last, according to what is told, who received his dignity on this stone.
>
> Now Edward King of England has conquered it, by the grace of Jesus Christ and by hard warfare. He offers it to St Edward like a king of great importance. Now he has passed by death, that no one can avoid.
>
> In Egypt Moses preached to the people. Scota, Pharaoh's daughter, listened well, for he said in the spirit, 'Whoso will possess this stone, shall be the conqueror of a very far-off land.'
>
> Gaidelon and Scota brought this stone, when they passed from the land of Egypt to Scotland, not far from Scone, when they arrived. They named the land Scotland from Scota's name.
>
> After Scota's death her husband took no other wife, but made his dwelling in the land of Galloway. From his own name he gave Galloway its name. Thus it appears that Scotland and Galloway are derived from their names.
>
> Now has Edward passed from this life, the conqueror of lands and flower of chivalry. Let us pray almighty God, who sways the whole world, that God may have mercy on his soul, God the son of Mary.

In this version, Scota and her husband go directly from Egypt to Scone without stopping off in Spain, Ireland or Argyll, all of which appear in later versions of the legend. Legge explains that the manuscripts may be abbreviated versions of the story. The original is known to have been quarried, along with other material, for somewhat creative versions of history.

Robertson explained how 'events which may have really happened are frequently misplaced and transferred to a wrong epoch, very often owing their misplacement to a wish to build up the fame of some favourite hero, by attributing to him the merit of every important action of several different periods. Scottish history abounds with instances of such misplacement.'

Professor Ted Cowan agrees. 'What concerns me is that the twelfth and thirteenth centuries were great periods for fabrications, inventions, substitutes, the manufacture of relics and so on. For example, shortly before the Stone business the Scots asked for the body of Malcolm Canmore to be returned from Alnwick where he'd been killed. The English chronicle says they just dug up some old English peasant and sent him, and the Scots were quite happy. The invention of tradition, where we were consciously trying to find things which were supposedly archaic and revive them, was very big in Ireland in this period, and I'm sure here, though we haven't spent much time on the subject yet.'

One of the oldest written references to the Stone comes from the time of Robert the Bruce. In 1301 the Scottish government was in direct competition with England for help from the Vatican. Desperate for recognition as an independent state, it commissioned the learned Canon Baldred Bisset of St Andrews to write up the history of Scotland in such a way as to 'prove' to Pope Boniface VIII that Scots had been converted to Christianity four centuries before the English, and that they had been civilised throughout the reigns of thirty-six kings while the English were still pagan. With this aim, Bisset set out a historical justification for the ancient right of Scotland to freedom from domination and presented it in Rome and, while Edward I was attempting to convince the bewildered Boniface that Scots descended from Alberactus, the *youngest* son of Brutus (the *Eponymus* of the Britons) the English came from the *eldest* and were therefore of greater importance, Canon Bisset was explaining how the daughter of Pharaoh, along with some Irish, had sailed to Scotland, taking with her the royal seat which Edward had so recently carried away by violence to England. He accused Edward of taking other significant items as well. The Canon further said that Scota conquered and destroyed the Picts and took and named their kingdom, tactfully massaging history into a more acceptable story, editing out an embarrassing expulsion of the Britons (English) by early Scots and blaming the Picts.

It worked. Pope Boniface preferred Baldred's story. Skene, who was not above adding and subtracting from history himself, says the whole story was fabricated. But would Canon Bisset actually have endangered his immortal soul by blatantly lying to the head of his Church? Is it not more likely that he re-orchestrated known details, ornamented with the occasional cadenza for effect?

Since these early accounts, written independently of each other, enjoy common features, Dominica Legge argued that Bisset did not invent his story, as Skene and Cowan suggested, 'but that a fairly extensive form of it was current in the thirteenth century'.

Variation in information about the size, shape and where-abouts of the original Stone creates controversy. Walter Hemingford, a late thirteenth-early fourteenth-century canon at Guisborough Priory in Yorkshire, wrote:

At the Monastery of Scone was placed a large stone in the church of God, near the great altar, hollowed out like a round chair, in which future kings were placed, according to custom, as the place of their coronation. [In Latin: *Apud Monasterium de Scone positus erat lapis pergrandis in ecclesia Dei, juxta manum altare, concavus quidem ad modum rotundae cathedreaie confectus, in quo future reges loco quasi coronationis ponebantur ex more.*]

This gave rise to the theory that the Stone of Destiny might once have been a Roman altar, a theory which will be examined in Chapter 7. Skene's research – 'Among the king's jewels which were in the castle of Edinburgh in 1296, was "*una*

petra magna super quam Reges Scotiae solebant coronari"
[a great stone upon which Scottish Kings were crowned]'
suggested, on the contrary, that the original Stone must
still be in Edinburgh, because the Westminster Stone is
so small.

We all read between the lines when we read history, adding
and subtracting according to our degree of scepticism, making
links according to our knowledge. Amateur historian Archie
McKerracher accuses Skene of turning 'academic somersaults'
in his enthusiastic efforts to prove Queen Victoria had been
rightfully crowned on the Stone.

McKerracher is particularly knowledgeable about the
Perthshire area and has long been interested in legends
about the Stone. He has looked at how it became known
as the Stone of Destiny, blaming misunderstanding on the
part of translators for theories such as, that the Stone of
Destiny was *Lia Fail*, the Oracle Stone used at the coronation
of the Irish High Kings which, in fact, 'remained on Tara
Hill until 1798'. Like all historians, he creates a theory:
the name 'Destiny' has come down to us 'due to a series
of errors', the prophecy '*Ni fallat fatum, Scoti quocunque
locatum, Invenient lapidem, regnare tenatur ibidem*' was
incorrectly copied by Boece from Fordun: instead of the noun
fatum Boece wrote *fatalis*, and Bellenden, who later translated
this for James V who couldn't read Latin, expressed *fatalis*
(badly) as 'fateful' – hence 'fatal' and 'fateful'. McKerracher
suggests, 'The Gaelic word *faileas* means a spiritual shadow
. . . it is the merest slip of a pen, or a mis-hearing, to render
that as *fail* – meaning fateful . . . From that somebody derived
"Destiny".'

By the sixteenth century the prophecy had taken this
form:

> The Scottis sall bruke
> that realme as native ground
> Gif weirdes [fates] faill nocht,
> quhairevir this chiar is found.

McKerracher discusses also the apparently nonsensical translation made by 'a gentleman' of the words found on one of the plaques discovered much later in Macbeth's Castle, Perthshire, and floats the suggestion that 'the dying Bruce had entrusted the Stone to Angus Og of the Isles to save it from the Balliols . . . One tradition says it lies in a cave behind a waterfall on Skye and the location is known today only to a family of MacDonalds, descendants of Angus Og, who are its hereditary custodians.'

The legend grows. McKerracher, like Skene, Boece, Fordun and the amiable Baldred Bisset, sifts nuggets from history, stirs in some educated guesswork, and comes up with tasty morsels of folklore. Through it all comes breathing the spirit of the people. Why has the legend persisted? Because it is boiled up from the bones of ancient fact.

The facts are these: early peoples did travel from Israel to Spain and Ireland. They used stones as ballast for their boats, which were capable of carrying quite heavy cargo, including large stone objects. There was a special Stone on which kings of the Scots were crowned. It was kept near the altar at Scone Abbey. It was extremely large. It had some kind of shaping, with a concave top. It was carved in some way. Edward I did take *a* block, cut from Perthshire sandstone, to Westminster in 1296.

The historian Marion Campbell noted in her book *Argyll, the Enduring Heartland* (1977), 'Legend will even tackle geological oddities; volcanic bubbles in a rock-sheet on the north shore of Loch Crinan have been explained as the hoof-marks of the horse on which Scota . . . rode ashore, bearing with her (as Nennius records) Jacob's Pillow'.

Legends are quarried by writers of fiction, and the first appearance of the Stone story being used in this way is *Scottish Chiefs* (1810), a charming little novel about William Wallace by an Englishwoman, Miss Jane Porter. Quoth her Earl of Monteith: 'the hallowed pillar [i.e. the Stone] was taken from Scone by the command of the king of England . . . The archives of the kingdom have also been torn from their sanctuary and were thrown by Edward's own hands into the fire.' Wallace responds: 'Scotland's history is in the memories of her sons; her palladium is in their hearts; and Edward may one day find that she . . . needs not talismans to give her freedom.' Wallace is then entrusted with an unusually heavy box – does it contain the Stone? Porter's footnote explains:

> Iber the Phoenician, who came from the Holy Land to inhabit the coast of Spain, brought this sacred relic along with him. From Spain he transplanted it with the colony he sent to people the south of Ireland; and from Ireland it was brought into Scotland by the great Fergus, the son of Ferchard. He placed it in Argyleshire; but MacAlpine removed it to Scone, and fixed it in the royal chair in which all the succeeding kings of Scotland were inaugurated. Edward I, of England caused it to be carried to Westminster Abbey, where it now stands. The tradition is, that empire abides where it stays.

Letters appear, written by people who mix vague memories of 1950-51 with scraps of history. The uncharitable might call them garbled tales. Actually they contain seeds of a new folklore which are being sown in the minds of the next generation.

The story of Scota and Gaythelus may be the folklore of How the Scots and the Gaels Got Their Names, but it is interesting to note how persistently certain parts of their story turn up, and from diverse sources. Simon Brec – not a particularly Spanish name – turns up with particular frequency.

'I argue that this is where all the peoples of dark age Scotland come together,' says Professor Cowan, 'in the tenth century, by rewriting the origin myths. So, instead of saying Scota the daughter of Pharaoh is the mother of the Scots, and the Picts descend from a prince of Scythia, Constantine says to his bards – right, we can solve this by writing a new origin legend – so what they come up with is that Scota was married to the Prince of Scythia. Right away the Picts and Scots have a common source, and then you fit the Britons and the Angles into this model and you come up with a new legend that makes everybody agree that they share a common ancestry by the tenth or eleventh century. If I'm right, that they were consciously into nation-forming that early, then of course ritual sites, inauguration stones and all the rest should be a concern at the same period and it all falls together.'

At Coldstream in the Borders on 15th November 1996, two army Landrovers and a white transit van crossed the bridge from England to Scotland amid much ceremony, politicians toasting each other in whisky to the skirl of the pipes. The watching crowd had been told the Stone of Destiny was inside one of the vehicles. But because no-one could see any stone, rumours rose from the whispers, like wind in the bracken: were we being duped again? How did we know the Stone – any stone – was being brought back to Scotland? The Coronation Stone must have been taken to Edinburgh weeks ago and we were being fobbed off with a khaki van. Within an hour this thought was being passed around as fact.

Professor Cowan confesses, 'I'm really interested just now in liminality, the study of boundaries: the boundary between our world and the other worlds, between a playing field that's for the players, and the other part that's for the spectators, the sacred space – for a football pitch is as sacred a space in a way, as an altar in a church.'

We don't like gaping holes in stories, so instinctively we cross the boundaries between fact and fiction, fill them in with invented reasons as we're driven to answer questions with suppositions, creative conclusions which the listener re-tells as truth. This need to link parts of a story provides the mesh upon which legend embroiders itself into such a winsome tapestry. Facts themselves are prone to interpretation – one has only to look at the way in which the Bible, which purports to be Truth, has been used. History is a magnificent quiz-show in which everyone can join.

CHAPTER FIVE

JACOB AND
THE THUNDER STONES

E very legend about the Stone tells us that it was once the
pillow on which Jacob had his dream.

Jacob, grandson of Abraham, lived around 1700 BC, at a
time when 'meteorites were believed to be very special', says
Dr Graham Durant, Curator of Mineralogy and Petrology at
the Hunterian Museum, Glasgow. The Greeks called them
'Thunder Stones' and most early peoples believed they had
supernatural powers. We know now that, from the asteroid
belt between Mars and Jupiter, two kinds of meteorites hurtle
towards us. What we see as shooting stars hit the earth's surface
with crater-making impact, the friction of their passage through
the atmosphere melting a smooth crust around the stony *aerolites*,
reducing *siderites* into petrified splashes of metal.

'There was little understanding of anything being outside
the Earth other than Heaven,' says Dr Durant. 'Not till
the eighteenth century were scientists able to explain their
true origin. Meteorites are either "finds" or "falls". Many
"finds" turn out only to be basalts with weathered crusts,
not meteorites at all. There's an example of polished basalt
in the Black Chair here in the museum.'

The Stone of Destiny is supposed to have been decorated with
carvings. If it was a meteorite, I asked Dr Durant, would people
living between, say, the era of Solomon (960 BC) and that of
Columba (AD 563) have had the technology to work it?

'Following the hypothesis that Jacob's pillow was described
as "stone", it must have been silicate – no different from
normal rock.'

But aren't meteorites usually quite small – about the size
of a tennis ball?

'Yes,' agreed Dr Durant, 'but they are occasionally huge.' In the eighteenth century a Russian blacksmith found one weighing 1600 lbs, which would have measured about three cubic feet, and in Thracia in 476 BC a Thunder Stone as large as a chariot fell to earth.

So it seems at least possible that Jacob found a suitably sized meteorite for his pillow, upon which marks of some kind could at some point have been carved.

Are there any precedents connecting meteorites and religion? The early Arabs worshipped gods who were thought to reside in sacred stones, trees and other elements of nature. The city of Mecca has always been their spiritual home, containing its famous building, the Kaaba (cube). In the eastern wall of the Kaaba, about five feet from the ground, is set a Black Stone. It is an aerolite which, well before the time of Muhammad, flashed through the sky and landed near an encampment of Arabs. They then made it an object of reverence. Muhummad was born around AD 570 into a clan of the Quraish tribe, Bedouins who ruled Mecca and had custodianship of the Kaaba and its Stone.

Stone was used in Israel to mark special places. It could withstand desert storms, great heat and great cold. Being heavy, it could not easily be stolen or displaced.

The honour Jacob accorded his pillow-stone shines through the King James translation of the Old Testament. In Genesis 28, Jacob was travelling from Beer-sheba to Haran when, at sunset, he

> took of the stones of that place, and put them for his pillows, and lay down in that place to sleep. And he dreamed, and behold a ladder set up on the earth, and the top of it reached to heaven: and behold the angels of God ascending and descending on it. And, behold, the Lord stood above it, and said, I am the Lord God of Abraham thy father, and the God of Isaac: the land whereon thou liest, to thee will I give it, and to thy seed; And thy seed shall be as the dust of the earth, and thou shalt spread abroad to the west, and to the east, and to the north, and to the south . . . And Jacob awaked out of his sleep, and he said, Surely the Lord is in this place; and I knew it not . . . This is none other but the house of God, and this is the gate of heaven.

> And Jacob rose up early in the morning, and took the stone
> that he had put for his pillows, and set it up for a pillar, and
> poured oil upon the top of it. And he called the name of that
> place Beth-el ... And Jacob vowed a vow, saying ... this stone,
> which I have set for a pillar, shall be God's house ...

Jacob set his pillar up as a permanent landmark, so that he
would recognise the place. In pouring oil on it he was making
a sacrifice.

Stones continued to be important to Jacob. He fell in love
with his cousin Rachel, a pretty shepherdess, when he helped
her move 'a great stone' which covered the well she wished to
use. Thus began the polygamous relationship with his uncle's
family and their servants that was to start a dynasty. Rachel
produced a son, Joseph.

Twenty-two years later God told Jacob to return to Beth-el,
where he re-named him Israel and said 'a company of nations
shall be of thee, and kings shall come out of thy loins; And
the land which I gave Abraham and Isaac, to thee I will give
it, and to thy seed after thee'. Jacob's response, again, is to
celebrate by setting up a stone pillar and making a sacrifice.

Soon after, near Bethlehem, Rachel went into a difficult
labour. Another son, Benjamin, was born, but Rachel died.
'Jacob set a pillar upon her grave', marking it with a stone
'that is the pillar of Rachel's grave unto this day'. At Shechem,
towards the end of his life, Jacob told his twelve sons – some
of whom had turned out better than others – that each would
start one of the tribes of Israel, giving Zebulun charge of the
seaboard, and Dan the power of judgement. Yet in Judges 5,
Deborah the prophetess asks 'Why did Dan remain in ships?'
suggesting that it was Dan who went to sea.

Much later Joshua, the successor of Moses, called his tribes
together in Shechem, to make a new law, and he 'took a great
stone, and set it up there under an oak, that was by the sanctuary of the Lord. And Joshua said unto all the people, Behold,
this stone shall be a witness unto us; for it hath heard all the
words of the Lord which he spake unto us: it shall be therefore

a witness unto you, lest ye deny your God.' Shortly after this, he died, reputedly aged a hundred and ten. The Pillar Stone was again used as a witness in 2 Kings 23 when King Josiah 'stood by a pillar, and made a covenant' that he would be good to his people. The point is that stone was believed capable of witnessing important events – of hearing the spoken word.

The Shechem stone next appears in Judges 9, when a character called Abimelech murders seventy of his brothers and is rewarded when 'all the men of Shechem gathered together . . . and made Abimelech king by the plain of the pillar that was in Shechem'. After a plot that makes *Macbeth* look like a bedtime story, a woman sensibly drops a stone on Abimelech's head from a tower.

The men of Judah 'anointed David king' over them in 2 Samuel 2, about 1,000 BC, and the following chapter refers to 'the throne of David' being set up over Israel. When David lay dying, in 1 Kings 1, he ordered Zadok the priest and Nathan the Prophet to bring his son Solomon and 'anoint him there king over Israel . . . that he may come and sit upon my throne; for he shall be king in my stead.' Zadok duly anointed him with holy oil and all the people celebrated the fact that 'Solomon sitteth on the throne of the kingdom.' We are told unequivocally, 'Then sat Solomon upon the throne of David his father; and his kingdom was established greatly.' We read of this again in 1 Chronicles 29: 'Solomon sat on the throne of the Lord as king'. In this way, the practices of enthronement and anointing were established and, as we have seen in Chapter 3, are treated with the same degree of seriousness by the British today, still accorded the same pomp and ceremony.

About 950 BC Solomon built a beautiful house for himself of stone, wood and gold, in 1 Kings 6, 'with carved figures of cherubims and palm trees and open flowers, and overlaid them with gold fitted upon the carved work.' The art of carving stone had been practiced already for hundreds of years for the inscription of laws, as on the pillar of King Hammurabi of Babylon (c. 1800 BC).

Was stone ever used in Biblical coronations? 2 Kings 11 has seven-year-old Joash being brought secretly to the Temple in Jerusalem by Jehoiada the priest. With guards surrounding the place 'he brought forth the king's son and put the crown upon him . . . and they made him king, and anointed him; and they clapped their hands, and said, God save the king . . . and . . . behold, the king stood *by* a pillar, as the manner was'. Other translators have made this 'stood *on* a pillar'. Whichever place is chosen, a tradition was being kept that kings of Israel received their crowns in the Temple and in close contact with the Pillar Stone set there by their forefather.

Disaster struck Israel about 585 BC. The prophet Jeremiah had been imprisoned, for prophesying bad times for his people. Nebuchadnezzar of Babylon beseiged Jerusalem. Two years later it fell, he destroyed the town and looted the Temple's gold. The king, Zedekiah, escaped over his garden wall with some of his family, but Nebuchadnezzar's men caught up with him, killed his sons in front of him, put out his eyes and took him captive. There were now no male descendants of David's line left. But Nebuchadnezzar freed Jeremiah, who promptly rescued several items from the Temple – the Tabernacle and the Altar of Incense are mentioned – and hid them in a cave near Pisgah. He also rescued Zedekiah's daughters, one of whom was the Princess Tea, and with them fled to Egypt. The law of inheritance in Israel, since the time of Moses, had included the right of women to succeed to the throne. Princess Tea was of David's line, and of the blood royal. Having taken such care, would he have left the central item around which the Temple and his people's culture had been built – the Stone Pillar of Jacob?

Jeremiah's scribe, Baruch, wrote down his next prophecy: that Nebuchadnezzar now wanted Egypt and its Pharaoh.

At this point our refugees from the eastern Mediterranean, Jeremiah, Baruch and Princess Tea disappear from biblical history.

The Mediterranean had been a busy sea for at least 2,000 years. From Israel, the tribe of Dan turned out to be the seafarers, though the Greeks called all sailors 'Phoenicians' (red men) on account of their weather-beaten skins. By about 1500 BC the Phoenicians had built a chain of ports along the coastline through which they imported luxury goods from Europe and Africa such as ivory, gold, silver, silk, and rare dyes, and exported them as value-added manufactured items. They built long boats for warfare, rounder ones with curved prows and sterns, powered by a dozen oarsmen, for trading. By 585 BC, when Jeremiah and his friends were leaving Israel, the Phoenicians had ventured well beyond the Straits of Gibraltar, setting up colonies such as Gades (Cadiz) on Spain's Atlantic seaboard. From there, we now know through archaeology, they traded as far as Britain and Ireland. Their main Mediterranean base became Carthage, where they were finally extinguished by the Romans about 146 BC.

Jeremiah, Baruch and Tea had to escape from Egypt ahead of Nebuchadnezzar. Where else could they go but to sea – and who more likely to take them than the Phoenicians, the sea-faring people, the tribe of Dan?

Phoenician trading ship 600 BC

CHAPTER SIX

≈

IRELAND

At the northern edge of the Phoenicians' west-coast sea route, an old prophet landed in Ulster. He was given the title Ollam Fodhla because it means 'professor', 'doctor' or 'learned man' and he was made king because of his great wisdom, ascending the Irish throne in Anno Mundi 3236 (526 BC), remaining there for forty years, according to O'Cleary's *Leabhar Gabhala* or Book of Invasions and Conquests. He founded a School of Prophets at Tara, and made laws based on the Ten Commandments, 'by which the nations of Eri were ruled for 1000 years'.

Ollam Fodhla was accompanied by a princess and a scribe called Simon Brech. The princess brought with her a Harp – once the emblem of David, later the emblem of Ireland, which is said to be buried at Tara, where the great stone, the Lia Fail, was set up.

Who exactly were these people? Is it merely the desire to make connections that suggests links where there is nothing more than coincidence? Jeremiah, Princess Tea and Baruch fled from Egypt around 580 BC, and lo, an elderly prophet, a princess and a scribe turn up in Ulster in 520 BC.

Ireland is a particularly useful stepping-stone in this mythology, because its version of Christianity encouraged the Irish people to develop a written script. With its long history uninterrupted by serious Roman invasion, penetration by the English, or ecclesiastical Reformation, the resulting record is a rich repository of information.

Originally, tales of bygone days would have been declaimed after triumphal battles, chanted before the inaugurations of kings, and told around firesides to circles of wrapt listeners.

It was a long time before a sufficiently sophisticated script was devised to put some of these in writing. They appeared as four main myths, from which it is clear that the 'West', was regarded as the source of all wonders. 'The West' is taken now to mean the Iberian Peninsula – Spain.

Robert Graves connected the beginnings of the Celtic peoples with Greece, for the trail of monuments they left can be followed around the western seaboard of Europe. Of all the various arrivals, by far the most interesting, for the purposes of this quest, is the Tuatha De Danann – the Tribe of Dan.

The Tuatha De Danann sailed in on one of the main routes taken by communities expanding outward from the eastern Mediterranean. The Dan tribe of Irish mythology loved science, technology, poetry, art, medicine and philosophy. They were skilled hunters, musicians and iron-workers. To the more pragmatic, their arrival simply indicates the beginning of the Iron Age in Ireland, but talents like these have indeed come down through Irish and Scottish genes to the present day. The mythological Dans brought with them four treasures: the Sword of Nuada, fatal at every stroke; the fiery spear of Lugh, perpetually dripping blood; the inexhaustible Cauldron of Dagda; and the Stone of Destiny.

The first Danann king of Ireland, Nuada, lost a hand in battle with a tribe of immigrants called the Fomors (probably Belgians). Kings had to be perfectly whole so, in a magnificent gesture of reconciliation, he abdicated in favour of Bress, son of the Fomorian king. The name 'Bress' is of interest because it sounds not unlike 'Brec' or 'Baruch.'

The Danann were not the last race to arrive in Ireland. The ancestors of the Gaels arrived from Spain, led by Mile, after which there is a real mix-up between the Tuatha, the Milesians, various deities, some magic, a lot of Celtic dignity, and a few intermarriages involving Herculean tasks and lots of sex, until eventually they all settled down together. With their script they recorded genealogies, folktales, laws and sagas, creating one of the oldest literatures in Europe.

Yet none of the existing literature provides real clues to the Hill of Tara, in County Meath, one of Ireland's most sacred places. Tara's Gaelic name is *Rath na Riogh* – the Fort of Kings – and its sanctity goes far back beyond the Iron Age. All the major routes of ancient Ireland converged on this magnificent high and empty plateau, and Tara still radiates atmosphere. There is much excavation to be done, but archaeologists now agree that this was indeed the seat of the High Kings of Ireland. A bank once enclosed a low hill, from which there is an impressive view in all directions. On it stood the Lia Fail, the Stone of Destiny, which historian Peter Harbison describes as 'the most obviously phallic symbol of ancient Ireland, and a monument which stresses the ritual importance of the site'.

It is here that perhaps we have a link with Christianity. Harbison goes on: 'In the dim shadows where mythology and history converge, Tara seems to have been in the hands of a Leinster dynasty, the Laigin. But in the early records, one can glimpse their defeat at the hands of the Ui Neill, a dynasty which was to play an extremely important role in the first 500 years of christianized Ireland.' In 1899 a fort there known as the Rath of the Synods was excavated by a group who believed it contained the Ark of the Covenant, which had been brought to Tara by the daughters of Zedekiah, one of whom was named Tea and after whom they understood the site had been named – Teamhair is the Irish for her name – mutated, through usage, to 'Tara'.

Even the English realised the importance of the indigenous culture they eventually conquered. One English antiquarian, Vallencey, saved an ancient poem, translating it for an Irish grammar book he wrote in the eighteenth century, to help redress 'the repeated indignities of late years cast on the history and antiquities of this once famed and learned island . . .':

> Seven ladies of the chiefest quality
> Followed the fortunes of the stout Milesians
> When they resolved to conquer or to die.
> Tea, the virtuous queen of Heremon;
> Fial the confort of the brave Lughaidh;
> Fais was a princess of distinguished beauty,
> And the beloved wife of Un; and Sceine
> Was wedded to Amergin's princely bed;
> Liobhradh was the royal pride of Fuaid:
> Scota, the relict of the great Milesius,
> And Oghba, strictly chaste in widowhood.

No serious historian would dare to suggest that Zedekiah's daughter Tea could have married the Irish King Eochaid the Heremon. And yet – it is not impossible . . .

Ollam Fodhla was the first king to hold the Fes, or Parliament of Tara, and the first to ordain district chiefs in Ireland. Dare we link Simon Brech with Jeremiah's scribe Baruch, connect Tara with the Princess Tea who had passed through Egypt as the guest of Pharaoh on her flight from Nebuchadnezzar, the sole survivor of David's line? Could she have been given the eponymous name 'Scota' by later writers because she wed Eochaid the Heremon, became Queen of the 'Scots' as the Irish were then known, and mother to a royal Irish-Scottish dynasty? Probably not – but because none of this is either provable or disprovable as yet, we are free to dream.

People have been dreaming about all this for a long time. The Revd J. B. Bartnette, writing in the *Jewish Chronicle* of September 1872, was convinced that Ollam Fodhla was 'no less a personage than the prophet Jeremiah himself, who with a remnant of the tribe of Judha emigrated to Ireland at the time of the Babylonian captivity, and became the great reformer, law-giver and ruler in that famous Western Isle', and that 'he brought with him Jacob's Stone known in Ireland as Lia Fail, or Stone of Destiny'. That idea has not entirely disappeared. There was a tradition that this Stone was called 'fatal' because if an impostor placed himself on it in an attempt to make himself king, it would remain silent, whereas when a prince of the blood-royal sat on it, it would cry out, giving an infallible sign of his right to accede to the crown.

What happened to it? There is a stone built into the roof of Blarney Castle which is said to confer the gift of persuasive speech on anyone who should kiss it (you have to upend yourself beneath the parapet to do so). The official guide book claims that the Blarney Stone is a part of the Scottish Stone of Destiny which was given to one Brian Boru for his help in fending off an enemy. It remains as another example of a piece of rock credited with magic powers. Annually, thousands of visitors pay money to kneel, upend themselves and kiss it, demonstrating again how strongly we can feel about a chunk of rock, however ridiculous it must seem to the wholly rational.

The use of ritual stones in Ireland is well documented by archaeologists and historians. One such is the Turoe Stone, near Bullaun in Co Galway. It is a domed granite cylinder 1.68 metres high, dating from the last few centuries BC, carved with complex and beautiful curvilinear trumpet-ends, triskeles and stylised animal heads. Harbison says there is evidence that the designs may originally have been emphasised 'in a variety of colours'. He also suggests it was used as an oracle, like the Omphalos stone at Delphi.

By studying carvings like those on the Turoe Stone, anthropologists have been able to trace more accurately the sources of the Irish people from France, Spain, Belgium and Britain, and to corroborate the information in the Book of Invasions which makes Spain a staging post on the Celtic route to Ireland, as people moved northward in the wake of the Romans. The *Ora Maritima*, written by Avienus in the middle of the fourth century AD, contains elements of an early Greek voyage of exploration somewhere around the sixth century BC. He mentions the presence of Celtic tribes on the North Sea, and in France and Spain at that time. As the Roman occupation began to fade in Britain, trade developed across the Irish Sea and, by the end of the fifth century AD, the northern Irish, confusingly then known as the Scotti, were colonising Argyll, naming it after their own people the Dal Riata, and bringing with them their way of cutting Ogham inscriptions on stone, the earliest surviving form of Irish writing. Did they bring with them a piece of the true Lia Fail?

≈

CHAPTER SEVEN

ROMANS AND CHRISTIANS

S cholars have formed various theories about the Stone. Since the 1950s there has existed one school of thought which suggests that the Stone of Destiny was once a Roman altar.

The problem this theory attempts to solve has to do with the Irish version of the Lia Fail story. Their Stone is known to have remained at Tara till 1798, when it was removed to mark the burial place of the Croppers, Irish rebel-heroes. If the Lia Fail did not leave Ireland before the ninth century, from whence appeared the Scottish Stone of Destiny? As we have seen, one tradition says a small part of it was supposedly broken off and brought to Scotland, either with the early immigration to Dalriada, or with Columba to Iona. But if the Irish Lia Fail never reached Scotland, what other stones might have appealed to the Scottish people for the inauguration of their kings?

There is plenty of evidence that the early dwellers in central Scotland worshipped fetish stones. Might they not, therefore, have cast acquisitive eyes on the carved slabs which seemed to confer such success upon Roman worshippers? The Romans used stones for altars, distance signs and other permanent markers, leaving them littered around their walls, forts and marching stations. Over the six centuries between their departure and the arrival of Mac Alpin, one of these altar stones might well have been made into a cult object, as writer Janet B. Christie suggested in the 1950s.

Roman writers described Caledonian folk as wild barbarians, with their inter-tribal warfare and their brightly checked clothing. Julius Caesar and the historian Cornelius Tacitus both wrote about the 'Picti' – who communicated in pictures, both in their body-paint and on their stones. While Agricola was consolidating his position with a line of Roman forts on the Forth-Clyde line, and reaching north to the vast swamp of Stirling moss in AD 83, the Caledonians were rolling boulders from fortified hilltop duns, throwing spears at sea-faring attackers from stone-walled brochs, and squabbling among themselves in their crannogs (large wooden islands found in inland lochs). They didn't stand a chance against sophisticated Roman organisation and advanced weaponry.

Pictish prisoners leaked the information that a major attack was imminent. Much remains unclear, but it seems that a leader, named by the Romans 'Calgacus', ('Calgaich' or 'swordsman') at last persuaded his Caledonians to unite against their common predator. At the showdown, called Mons Graupius by Tacitus, near Bennachie, 30,000 fearless Caledonian warriors 'tall, fair or red-haired . . . in primitive tartan . . .their shields and helmets gay with enamel . . . followed by . . . half naked, barefoot infantry' hurled themselves suicidally at the Roman army.

Tacitus wrote: 'On the succeeding day, a vast silence all around, desolate hills, the distant smoke of burning houses, and not a living soul descried by the scouts', making out that Mons Graupius had been a great conquest. Yet Tacitus left Britain only months later, and the Romans trickled southwards till the arrival of Hadrian in 122; he stretched his wall from the Solway to the North Sea, marking the new limit of the Roman Empire.

Tired of constant trouble from the Caledonians, Hadrian's successor, Antoninus Pius, ordered another invasion. Accordingly, in 142, his governor, Lollius Urbicus, marched north to strengthen the wrecked forts of his predecessor and build the Antonine Wall. It was only partially effective for about twenty years. By the end of that century the Roman Empire in Britain, weakened by a terrible epidemic, poor leadership, corruption and an over-stretching of their resources, imploded. The joyous Caledonians quickly repossessed their territory.

Gloom shrouds the ensuing Dark Ages, but we know that,

while late in the fourth century Saxons were attacking the south east coast of Caledonia, the west was being raided by *Scotti* – the name means 'raiders' – fierce Irish warriors seeking slaves.

Did the Caledonians help themselves to artefacts from derelict Roman habitations? Throughout history, it seems, conquered people have held on to souvenirs of their occupation, so it is possible. That the Romans used places of worship along the Antonine Wall is without doubt. Several altars have been found and can be seen in the Hunterian Museum of Glasgow University. Christie made a study of these, suggesting that they resembled seats or chairs. Certainly any verbal depiction of them – the depression in the surface, the volutes at each side – match descriptions of the Stone. Christie's favourite Roman altar was found in 1771 at Castlecary to the east of the A80 near Falkirk, cut from local limestone, 15 inches high, its top 15 inches by 11 inches with volutes at each side 3 inches in diameter. In the centre is a round basin 7 inches in diameter and five-eighths of an inch deep. What is left of the pediment bears the inscription 'DEAE'. Persuasively, Christie argues that the complete altar might have been two to three feet high, and that the completed Latin inscription might have supported her theory.

In fact the proportion of most Roman altars is pedestal-like, tall and narrow – and there is no reason to believe this one would have been different when complete. Anyone sitting on top would look as though they were perched on an ornate bird-bath, their feet dangling several inches above the ground.

Dr Lawrence Keppie, Senior Curator of Archaeology and History at the Hunterian Museum, is 'not aware of any examples of altars or parts of them being carried away to Pictish or Scottish sites', though 'certainly stonework was removed for re-use ... for example at Jedburgh Abbey.' Dr Keppie suggests we consider instead the mysterious Black Stone which has been in the University of Glasgow since its foundation in 1451, which is now on view, set in an eighteenth century chair. There were once similar stones at Edinburgh and Aberdeen, and one remains at St Andrews. He says that 'These stones fall within a general category of ceremonial seats of which the Stone of Destiny is a conspicuous example.' Perhaps, all along, the Stone has been on public view!

There is one tenous trail of tradition that links the Stone of Destiny with the little towns of Whithorn and Melrose in the south of Scotland. Whithorn lies three miles from the end of a headland jutting southward into the Solway Firth, and has clearly been regarded as a particularly holy place for a very long time. Local place-names reverberate with ancient sounds: the Mote of Druchtag, the Doon of May, the Standing Stones of Drumtrodden, and St Ninian's Cave. The peninsular tip, the 'Isle' of Whithorn, has always embraced a harbourful of ships, having been an important haven since the earliest times, and a little ruined chapel sits by the bay on which visiting pilgrims used to land.

Christianity had been declared the official state religion of the Roman Empire in the fourth century, by Constantine the Great. Evangelistic monks travelled far and wide to preach it. The Venerable Bede (673-735), who finished his *Ecclesiastical History of the English Nation* in 731, tells us

> these southern Picts ... received the faith of truth, when the word was preached to them by Nynia, a most reverend bishop and holy man of the nation of Britons, who had been regularly instructed at Rome in the faith and mystery of the truth ... The place, which belongs to the province of the Bernicians, is called in the vernacular 'At The White House', he there built a church of stone in a manner to which the Britons were not accustomed.

Galloway was a natural stopping-place on the ancient sea-route from the Mediterranean and Spain to the Northern Isles and Norway and, as the Romans left these shores, Christian missionaries were infiltrating the area. Little is known of Ninian, but his relics, or preserved remains, were revered. Lost in the Reformation, found again, the final bone which had been encased in silver by King James IV, turned up in the chapel of the Scots Seminary at Douai in Belgium, where it was last seen in 1785 by Carruthers, a priest from Dumfries.

One of the earliest Christian stone monuments in Scotland was discovered near Whithorn. Inscribed in Latin: 'We, Latinus, 35 years, and his daughter, 4 years, praise the Lord. The grandson Barrovadus set up this memorial.' It dates from the mid-fifth century AD, well before Kenneth Mac Alpin's time, and demonstrates that special stones were being carved in Scotland.

Archaeologists, who have been working on the site under Dr Peter Hill since it was rediscovered in 1984, have found low walls that mark the site of a chapel which is almost 1300 years old. They have found pieces of amphorae (wine jars) from the East Mediterranean, table-ware from North Africa, French cooking vessels and fine drinking glasses, all fifth century luxury items that demonstrate the wealth and prestige that once appertained to Whithorn. Every year from April till October teams of archaeologists work on this magnificent dig, where they welcome and inform interested members of the public. The Whithorn Trust Museum shows the latest finds.

Close by the chapel, people have been burying their dead ever since its beginnings, and because of the anaerobic conditions of the soil some of the remains are remarkably well preserved. Skeletons of people who, during lifetime witnessed the visits of many famous Scots, have been laid bare, their graves measured and any scraps of clothing or possessions conserved. The very teeth that must have smiled at Robert the Bruce on his last pilgrimage are still in existence.

Whithorn survived the Viking raids. St Ninian's Shrine became a focus for pilgrims from Europe, who regarded the journey as a spree as well as a penance. Just as in Lourdes today, places of pilgrimage drew wealth from their visitors. But the little town suffered bad times too, such as when the cathedral and the town were burned to the ground in 1286.

That Bruce did visit Whithorn is historical fact. He was fifty-four and suffering a life-threatening disease. In 1328 the Pope had withdrawn his excommunication, which gave him a measure of psychological relief. He set out on pilgrimage to St Ninian's Shrine in February 1329 in order to make his peace with God, for it had been near a kirk dedicated to St Ninian that he had enjoyed his greatest triumph, at Bannockburn. After a difficult journey through the biting cold, he reached Whithorn on 1st April. He spent four or five days there, praying and fasting, before making his painful way home.

What does any of this tell us? That Whithorn was a much-frequented port, Christianised very early. It had strong links with all the places through which Jacob's Pillow is believed to have travelled. Stones of importance were carved in the area from the earliest times. Whithorn was one of the landfalls used by travellers from Ireland to Edinburgh. Its monastery was one of a chain across lowland Scotland, which included Melrose and Lindisfarne. Whether or not an important stone passed through Whithorn in the early days we do not know, but Whithorn, as an important religious centre, did connect with Melrose and other monasteries.

In response to a request for information circulated to newspapers throughout Scotland, a postcard arrives. Written in capitals, it reads: 'The black oblonged piece rock which came from Ireland by St Ninian in 803 A.D. is buried 12 ft below the altar in Melrose Abbey. The stone in London which is the same size is a faked' [sic]. This may well be another mixture of half-digested material – witness the incorrect date given for St Ninian – but is exactly how legend grows, and therefore merits brief investigation. Very possibly it will lead down a blind alley, or perhaps it will alert us to something we have not before considered.

The original monastery of *Mailros* referred to by Bede in 731 had been founded by St Aidan a century earlier with monks brought from Iona via Lindisfarne, three miles east of the present Abbey. One of the earliest priors was Cuthbert, who lived there before taking over as prior of Lindisfarne, on which Mailros was dependent. David 1 (1124 -53) found the site unsuitable, and according to the *Chronicle of Melrose* – a record written by the monks living there – the new abbey was consecrated on Sunday 28th July 1146. Generations of Scottish monarchs patronised the Abbey and it became one of the richest monasteries in the kingdom. Alexander II had himself interred there even though he died near Oban in 1249, and Robert the Bruce was known to have an affection for it. Kings of England, notably Edward I, sacked it over and over again and Bruce kept rebuilding it, doing everything in his power to get God on his side in spite of his excommunication. In a letter addressed to his son dated 1329 he asked him to see that the rebuilding of Melrose continued, and to make sure his heart was buried there when he died.

Melrose Abbey is built from rose-coloured sandstone quarried from the nearby Eildon hills. Lofty arches still bear the most intricate carvings and traceries. Looking skyward the eye is caught and held by strange little human faces carved high on the walls. Much of the best work was done by the Parisian stone mason John Morrow, who introduces himself in carved letters on his tombstone thus: *John Morow sum tyme callit was I and born in Parysse* [Paris] *certainly and had in kepyng all mason werk of Santandroys* [St Andrews] *ye hye kyrk of glasgw* [Glasgow] *melros* [Melrose] *and paslay* [Paisley] *of nyddysdayll* [Nithsdale] *and of galway I pray to God and Mari baith and swete Sanct Johne to kepe this haly kirk fra skathe* [harm]. Morrow is claimed as the first Master of the Freemason Lodge at Melrose, one of the oldest in Scotland.

The ruined skeleton of Melrose Abbey now springs from trim gardens where the old monastery walls are bedecked with climbing roses in red, gold and white, entwined with purple clematis. On a sunny day in summer it basks in the appreciation of busloads of tourists, but there is a darker side to Melrose, too, as a succession of its custodians will testify.

Jimmie Blain has been Custodian of Melrose Abbey for twelve years. Local people ask Jimmie if he has yet been visited by the White Lady, who seems to have given him a wide berth so far. But he tells of areas within the oldest parts of the Abbey where, when he or one of his workers is raking the gravel, a different sound is wont to echo beneath their feet. He wonders what archaeologists will find, when eventually these hollow depths are dug. One evening recently, after the crowds had gone and just before closing time, a family group arrived with their dog on its leash. Jimmie accompanied them, chatting about the Abbey's past, their feet crunching on the gravel. Just inside the West entrance of the Nave – where the hollow sound is heard – the dog stopped, its hackles rising. Nothing its owners could do would persuade their dog to cross that patch. It stood rooted to the ground, shivering and whimpering with fear. What strange object lies beneath? Could it include the old Stone of Destiny?

Melrose Abbey undoubtedly houses the mortal remains, and possibly therefore the shades, of some remarkable individuals. When the 1888 guidebook was written by Mr J. Wass, the custodian of that time, the heart of Robert the Bruce was believed to lie buried beneath the High Altar in the Chancel at the easternmost end of the Abbey. But then so are the mortal remains of Michael Scott, the Wizard credited with separating the nearby Eildon Hills into three.

A recent letter from George Smith, retired custodian, states: 'About the black stone under the High Altar, there is no specific mention of it in any books or charters. However it is my belief that after the destruction of the Abbey in 1385 when the much revered black marble Holy Rood was broken, a piece of it was saved and buried under the High Altar when the Abbey was being rebuilt.'

The Black Rood of St Margaret, in its gilded silver case, was looted from Edinburgh Castle by Edward I along with the

Stone of Scone in 1296, but unlike the Stone, it was returned. David II (1329-71) lost it at the battle of Nevill's Cross, but the Black Rood later found its way to Durham Cathedral, disappearing from there at the Reformation. But would such a venerated relic really have disappeared? We have followed the vicissitudes of several others, and somebody, somehow always seems to have spirited them into safety.

Local tradition, passed down the generations, yet again inspired historians' curiosity. They found that something of interest did indeed lie hidden beneath the altar. Some years ago excavators found a mummified heart in a leaden casket. As they could not at that time positively identify it, they re-interred it. In 1996 it was rediscovered and examined by Historic Scotland, who will not declare it to be the Bruce's heart, though many are convinced that it is (see Chapter 14 below).

No Stone of Destiny has so far been found at Melrose. And yet there are odd connections. George Smith reminds us that 'the Knights Templar have a stone in their keeping which they claim is the original one'. Melrose has links with the Knights Templar, as we shall see later. What connection has Melrose with Whithorn?

There was only one individual who was possessed of a deep reverence for Whithorn, a love of Melrose, sufficient wealth to help preserve both places, the motivation to visit both in person on many occasions, a connection with the Knights Templar, and secret knowledge of the whereabouts of the Stone of Destiny, and that person is none other than Robert the Bruce himself.

The Stone of Destiny, then, may just possibly have been a Roman altar. It seems marginally more likely that it could have been brought into Scotland via Whithorn as a holy object along with the earliest Christians. Whatever the truth, we know there's still a mystery at Melrose.

≈

CHAPTER EIGHT

DALRIADA AND
THE ROYAL BOAR

Many people believe that the Stone of Destiny came to Scotland from Ireland along with some of the early immigrants. These people came in through the lochs and rivers with which the western seaboard of Scotland is indented. One of these ancient waterways led in through what is now Loch Crinan to the fortress of Dunadd, capital of the ancient kingdom of Dalriada – now western Argyll.

Marion Campbell, whose family roots reached far back in Argyllshire history, wrote lovingly of the flat, fertile land that lies between Lochgilphead and Crinan. For her the very name A'Mhoine Mhor (the Big Moss) 'has the sough of winds in it'. Near the north-eastern end of A'Mhoine Mhor, Dunadd 'crouches like a great lion' almost two hundred feet above the present sea-level. Its causeway is now a farm track 'down which have gone the feet of spear-men, riding-ponies, pack-horses and royal chariots, for it was once the high road to a capital.' Nowadays one will always encounter one or two people on the road, for it draws both the curious passer-by and the expert.

The river Add wanders westward from its source in Loch Sitheanach (loch of the fairy mound) high in the hills between Loch Awe and Loch Fyne, coiling lazily round the foot of the rock in shiny black curves, meandering on to Loch Crinan, a slip of silver in the distance. Campbell writes:

> The tide itself once washed where now the mist lies, at the lip of a shelf carved by cold seas out of glacial drift, in that long age when land and sea played a slow see-saw and the rocks escaped from their vast ice-coffin. That was before the hunters

came northwards from the lands where their far ancestors had caught Rhone salmon or chased the wild bulls of Altamira. When the first man trod this ground is still an unanswered question; perhaps he came towing a sledge and hooded in deerskin to fish among the floes where the fat shoals swam; perhaps he traversed bleak tundra from pocket to stunted pocket of scrub-willow; perhaps already he braved the open sea ... When the ice-fed sea was highest it made a bay of Crinan Moss and an inlet of Glassary Glen ...

Archaeologist Ronald Morris agrees with Campbell that until somewhere between 2000 and 1500 BC, the sea was indeed higher than it is now, 'perhaps by about 25 ft', which helps us to date the earliest of the carvings, and to tell us that the people who made them came by sea and were 'perhaps among the very first inhabitants when our Scottish land became really inhabitable after the last ice age ended.'

An old local tradition claims that ships once berthed at the base of the rock. Here were found the shattered remains of red Samian ware – pottery the Romans used – and of Gaulish wine jars. Adamnan wrote of the French wine ships coming 'to the head of the region'. As boar expert and Greenwich scholar Patrick Carnie explains, the curraghs plying between Ireland and Scotland, sturdy skin-covered boats, were capable of carrying the Stone of Destiny or any other large stone. Like the Phoenicians, their sailors used boulders as ballast.

In the years between 500 and 800 Dunadd was the most important stronghold of Dalriada. Celtic tribes would often fortify a hill central to their territory, to use as their capital, and for the inauguration of their kings.

Campbell takes us up the steep climb from the causeway, through a cleft in the rock a hundred feet above the plain. 'Here, within a massive girdling wall, is a green level strewn with hut-ruins and a well whose spring now supplies the farm below. A grass-grown stairway leads to higher terraces, the topmost of them still bearing part of a curved citadel-wall, and below it to the northward a bare sheet of rock.' This outcrop bears six worn carvings: a deep cup surrounded by a faint ring, an excised line-drawing of a boar, and two footprints, one clearly defined size 8 and another, more shadowy. There is also Ogham script. The Dal Riata used this simple form of writing, slash marks starting from a single line, which can still be seen quite clearly in the shadows produced by low sun at Dunadd.

After sitting quietly in its moss for a thousand years, Dunadd returned to the attention of the public through the researches of Skene in 1850. In Victorian times, archaeology was still in its infancy. Too frequently clumsy excavation destroyed stratification – the layers which denote different periods of occupancy. Amateur archaeologists were inclined to take home, then often lose, artefacts. The Society of Antiquaries of Scotland carried out digs at Dunadd in 1904-5 and 1929, but learned little from the exercise.

Most of what we do know of the early days at Dunadd comes from Irish writings. The earliest Irish annals, dating from around 563 to about 740, were written long after the events to which they refer, but their source was oral tradition, passed down from generation to generation in the way we have described. In this case the annals tell of a small kingdom on the coast of County Antrim whose people were migrating to Argyll by the fifth century. They had a leader called Reuda, or Riata. Fergus son of Erc, a contemporary of St Patrick, ruled the Dal Riata people in Ireland, and is believed to have established authority over this area of Argyll. He died in 501, having started a dynasty that would expand Dalriada to the borders of the British kingdom of Dumbarton on the shores of the river Clyde, and eventually to the Pictish kingdoms of the north and east. The descendants of his grandsons Gabran, and Comgall who gave his name to the Cowal peninsula, surface into history during the eighth century.

Whoever founded Dalriada, by this time their descendants had also fortified duns at Dunaverty, Tarbert, and Dunollie, near Oban. There were years of uncertainty – Dunadd was beseiged in both 683 and 736 – but eventually a new name emerges from the misty Dalriadic descendants. It is that of Kenneth Mac Alpin. And Mac Alpin is believed to have had quite a bit to do with the Stone of Destiny.

The practice of incising rock had existed in Scotland already over a long period. Morris wrote: 'over three thousand five hundred years ago, an unknown race of men began, for the first time in the British Isles, to carve on stone.' These early carvings of hollows, squiggles, circles and spirals known as cups and rings still puzzle archaeologists. In Argyll alone there are about eighty sites, forty-seven of which are near Dunadd. There are certain constants in these carvings. They are found on movable slabs and often occur also on 'the living rock' – outcrops that form part of the underlying geological structure. Carvings on outcrop rock are usually 'within 20 degrees of horizontal', set where there is an open view of a waterway. Most are within walking distance, about six miles, of places where gold or copper ore was once extracted. All of these conditions are fulfilled at Dunadd, where jewellers and fine metalworkers plied their trade.

At present, archeologists believe rock carvings had ritualistic significance, to do with the sun, for ceremonies such as burial, for practical purposes to do with astronomy and metal prospecting, and for the inauguration of kings. The practice of placing a new king's foot or feet in specially carved-out 'footprints' has been discussed in Chapter 3. One can envisage the rising sun illuminating the new king after his night-long vigil, the cup full of oil, or blood, for sacrifice or for anointing him. Campbell notes that the footprints are 'so placed that anyone who stands in them faces the distant crests of Cruachan . . . fourteen hill-forts stand within sight of Dunadd . . . from their walls the shields flashed in salute and the hilltop fires blazed out on coronation night'.

The Dal Riata of Dunadd organised their society according to principles of law which were to become fundamental in Scotland. Campbell explains:

Celtic kings were probably, like any other primitive king, half-divine; on their courage and integrity depended the health of the people and the fruitfulness of the land; but they were not absolute monarchs. They remained subject to the law (as indeed the Crown in Scotland is still under the laws and can be sued through its ministers), and the law was in the hands of a class of highly-trained jurists, the *Breitheamhan*, men of the priestly caste which stood above the warrior-caste from which the kings were drawn.

To reach this rank you had to pass through a strenuous training, in which nothing was written and everything had to be committed to memory. If you passed through all three of the mysterious seven-year-long training periods you became what the Roman writers called a Druid.

It is thanks to St Patrick that any fragments of the law were written down. He selected only those laws that did not conflict with Christianity, and these still pertained until the medieval period in Scotland. Contract is the fundamental principle, whether between God and man, king and people, or man and woman. Intention of offence is punishable, and every breach of contract is healed by appropriate compensation. Failure to make good a breach of contract resulted in outlawry, the worst punishment, because the individual banned from the group is without protection. A king inaugurated on Dunadd was entering into a contract with his people, and a contract with God.

The Dunadd Ogham, though Irish in type, has not yet proved fully translatable, which makes it more akin to the enigmatic Oghams of the Picts. The boar carving, too, is a Pictish symbol, while lacking certain features that would make this attribution definite. These two pieces of evidence suggest some Pictish connection with Dunadd. The Picts communicated through a whole vocabulary of animals, birds, fish and serpents as well as strange symbols. Professor Duncan suggests that some of these symbols represent objects used in the first century, and that they were depicted on perishable materials or in tattoing till the period in which they appear on stone. The carvings are believed to denote the identity of great warriors or leaders, each symbolised by a particular animal deity with whom the ancestor of the commemorated person was associated. Who was symbolised by a boar? Possibly Angus I, an early king of Picts who either conquered the Dal Riata or merged with them. Is it not likely that the ancestral symbol of a Pictish king would be carved on any Stone used at his inauguration too?

At Dunadd, therefore, there is clear connection with Ireland, with Irish kings, their king-making ceremonies and religions. The sea-route to Ireland had been used since the earliest times. The Dal Riata were highly artistic and skilled. They made rock carvings, and used existing ones. The summit rock shows workmanship of periods spanning 2000 years. Are the Dal Riata likely to have left behind in Ireland their special Stone – one reputedly blessed by St Patrick himself? Is it not possible that they would have brought a part of it with them?

In a society for whom art and carving on rock were a normal means of communication, as well as an important part of their king-making ceremonies, it would at least appear likely that a venerated object such as the Stone of Destiny would be richly decorated with carvings and colour.

CHAPTER NINE

COLUMBA, KING OF STORMS

Legends about the Stone of Destiny tell us that it was either St Columba's pillow or his altar, connecting it with the Hebridean island of Iona. We should therefore take a look at how and why sixth century monks such as Columba used these stones.

Many people have written about Columba. The first to do so was Cuimine the Fair, Abbot of Iona just sixty years after Columba's death. Later Adamnan quarried Cuimine's work for his own 'life' of the saint. Peering through the hagiographic mists, in which Adamnan 'proves' how the saint's life was pre-destined in the Bible, we search almost in vain for Columba the individual.

His birth is heralded by an angel which appears to his mother Eithne in a dream and presents her with an exquisite cloak glowing with the colours of all the flowers in creation. She is to bear a son of great beauty:

> A youth shall be born out of the north
> With the rising of the nations;
> Ireland shall be made fruitful by the great flame,
> And Alba, friendly to him.

And, it goes on, he is to be remembered throughout history. This gives us a clue to medieval thinking. These early Christian evangelists liked to emulate the behaviour of their biblical predecessors, and those who wrote about them later liked to confirm their likeness to Really Holy People by showing that they lived in the same way. Accordingly, Columba's birth is announced like the birth of Christ, and he has a Jacob-type dream on the pillow-stone which was later set up to mark his grave. Columba is quite likely to have slept on stone, genuinely to follow his hero Jacob, so here Adamnan may well have been documenting fact. He had at his disposal both written and oral sources. People living at the time of Columba were also accustomed to seeing stone and wood and metal that had been carved into intricate and beautiful designs, first pagan, later with Christian symbols added, and we can take it that he was familiar with such art.

Columba was born in Gartan, Donegal, it is said, on Thursday 7th December 521, and his life must indeed date from about that year. His clan, the royal Ui Neill mentioned in Chapter 6, ruled the north of Ireland from Tara and Armagh, both ancient centres of Druid activity. Art historian Ian Finlay writes of the ritual stone heads which can still be seen in Armagh cathedral, and at Tara, of 'the Stone of Fal, a phallic monument which vented a shriek in the presence of a rightful king' which, as we have seen, remained there till the eighteenth century.

Columba, then, grew up among carved and magic stones. Yet although eligible, Columba was not groomed for kingship. Instead he was given in fosterage to Cruithnechan, a priest, and baptised with the name of the dove for peace, perhaps as a family offering to the church. The practice of sending a child into fosterage was normal at that time, and the resulting relationships became as close as blood-ties. He studied under some of the greatest teachers of his day, and he was clearly what we call especially gifted. After his ordination, he spent fifteen years preaching around Ireland and founding monasteries such as Durrow.

In spite of his peaceful name, Columba was a stirring fellow. Tradition says he caused the terrible battle of Cooldrevne (561), Ireland. Many were killed. For this sin his sentence should have been excommunication but either St Molaisi intervened, or he imposed the penance on himself: perpetual exile from his native country. Finlay writes 'One grasps at straws as pointers to the truth, and the only wisp is the celebrated *Cathach*', a psalter which Columba allegedly copied against the wishes of his superiors. It still exists, in Dublin.

At any rate, in 563, for meteorological reasons most likely in early summer, Columba set off across the sea with twelve companions. After a journey of a hundred miles, his boat grounded on a steep pebble beach now called Port a Churaich (port of the Coracle), at the south end of the island known then as I or Y, now as Iona. He climbed the highest nearby hill. Ireland had disappeared below the blue line of the horizon. In 1798 we first hear of the tradition that he placed a stone on the spot, which is still called Carn Cul re Eirinn (Cairn of the Back to Ireland), but this cairn looks too modern. The same place name appears on Oronsay and Mull and is now thought perhaps to date from the old boundaries of Dalriada.

Whether or not it is true that Columba brought part of the Lia Fail as a parting gift from Tara, he may well have brought his own altar. These travelling altars were sometimes made of stone, and occasionally of stone imported from the Holy Land.

What did Columba find on arrival on Iona? The prospect from Carn Cul re Eirinn is not very promising, but as he and his companions wandered northwards through the wildflowers and butterflies of the machair, the island's character unfolded before them. It is an island full of magic stones. Green is its main colour, the green of sea grasses and pasture, fringed with white sands to the north, buttressed against storms raging northwards up the Irish Sea by rocky headlands and jagged gullies where knobs of translucent green marble roll and tumble in the surf. Measuring only about four miles by two, its highest hill, Dun I, measures 332 feet above sea level. Columba was not the first human being to dwell in this small Eden; there is plenty of Bronze Age, Iron Age and Stone Age evidence of earlier lives.

He and his monks evolved a simple life. He lived in a beehive-shaped cell built of smooth stones from the shore covered with a wooden framework and a turf roof, which he called 'my little hut', and which was situated 'on the higher ground', believed to have been the rocky mound of Tor Abb, on which evidence of early building has been found. He and his faithful attendant Diormit were on good terms. There was a bell which he could ring to summon the other monks, and they sang prayers in their little church. They wore sandals and, for special festivals, white robes. Sometimes Columba would write in his cell, sometimes he would go on retreat to another island he called Hinba. This may have been Eilean-na-Naoimh, the furthest west island of the Garvellachs in the Firth of Lorne, on which beehive cells still exist. Here he would fast, pray and sing. He also travelled throughout Scotland, weaning people away from their pagan practices, which usually involved a lot of power vested in the Druids who ruled by making people fear them. Columba's religion must have seemed wonderful – downgrading personal power, preaching kindliness to your neighbour and promising a glorious afterlife, especially if the present one was proving difficult.

During this time, so the legend goes, Columba became closely involved in the affairs of two kings. One of these was Bridei mac Maelchon, who ruled in eastern Pictland – a long and dangerous journey away. Bridei's stronghold sat somewhere between Loch Ness and the North Sea, either on the rocky knoll inside Castle Urquhart, or on the hillfort of Craig Phadrig, to the north of present-day Inverness. Perhaps he had heard of Columba's miraculous powers and hoped these might help him overcome the Druids. Adamnan describes conflict from the moment Columba arrived. The Druids, led by Bridei's sick old tutor Broichan, attempted to 'cause' a great storm that would prevent Columba from sailing his small boat up 'the long lake of the river Nesa'. When Columba succeeded in reaching Bridei's palace he demonstrated mercy by instantly curing him with a white stone from the Ness, which he later presented to him to ward off death. Stone was clearly useful to Columba. Again, one day while he was crossing the Ness, he found some people 'burying an unfortunate man, who ... was a short time before seized as he was swimming, and bitten most severely by a monster that lived in the water.' He persuaded one of his monks to strip off and leap into the water as bait. 'The monster ... suddenly rushed out, and, giving an awful roar, darted after him with its mouth wide open.' But Columba made the sign of the cross, commanding the monster to leave the monk and 'to return to the deep ... At the voice of the saint, the monster was terrified, and fled more quickly than if it had been pulled back with ropes.' We're told Bridei was delighted, but in fact the conversion of the north didn't get under way till well after 700. According to Adamnan, Bridei kept his stone as a souvenir, and the monster was not seen again till the camera was invented. Now Nessie is no longer fierce, and kindly sees to it that many people are gainfully employed in the Inverness area who might otherwise have had to leave the country.

Columba helped the second king more reluctantly. After some sort of mental struggle out on his retreat island of Hinba, during which he got badly scourged by an angel because he wanted to appoint his friend Iogenan to the kingship of Dalriada, he was forced to ordain Iogenan's brother Aidan instead – and so badly was he wounded that he carried the scar for life.

The historians get busy now. Skene writes about the inauguration of Aidan:

> St Columba had obtained at the Council of Dumceat the independence of Scotch Dalriada; and if ever there was an occasion on which the Stone of Destiny might be expected to play a prominent part, it was in the solemn rite by which St Columba constituted Aidan King, in obedience to a divine command declared in a vision, and accompanied by a prophecy regarding his successors. He ordains him by placing his hands upon his head, blessing him, using what Adamnan calls '*verba ordinationis*;' but, throughout the whole description, there is not a single allusion to the Fatal Stone.

Skene says that the theory of his contemporary historian, Robertson, 'by which he endeavoured to reconcile the non-appearance of the stone in the inauguration of the Scottish kings of Dalriada with the legend which makes Kenneth Mac Alpin bring the stone from Argyllshire to Scone in the ninth century, was enthusiastically adopted by Dean Stanley in his *Historical Memorials of Westminster Abbey*', but sums up the argument: 'Both Cumine and Adamnan speak of a stone at Iona which had been used by St Columba as a pillow, and on which he rested his head in his dying hours, and the first shape in which the legend of the stone of Scone meets us is as the pillow of Jacob . . . Columba had a vision of angels before his death' – just like Jacob.

The Pictish Chronicle records that Kenneth Mac Alpin, in the seventh year of his reign, transported the relics of St Columba to a church which he built on the banks of the river Tay, and Skene suggests that the stone pillow may have been included.

Finlay, the art historian, says of the Monymusk Reliquary, thought to have contained the physical relics of the saint when they were taken to Dunkeld, that it had enormous importance, for there was a tradition that if it be carried thrice, sunwise, around an army of Columba's people, victory would be theirs. This is evidence of a pagan idea being overlaid with Christianity.

Through all the speculation, glimpses of Columba's character, his reactions to events, and a few facts, emerge. We know that he was indeed in the habit of sleeping on a flagstone with his head on another stone, whether or not in deliberate imitation of Jacob. This must have been very uncomfortable, even if they were padded with bracken, rushes or heather, yet it was probably drier than the earth itself. Mortification of the flesh may have been considered good for the soul, but a crippled Columba would not have been much use as an itinerant preacher; by no stretch of the imagination could he have had for his pillow a rock measuring the size of the chunk of sandstone that lies beneath the coronation chair at Westminster today, let alone something high enough for a future Scottish king to sit on with dignity, without running a risk of seriously slipping a disc.

On Iona local people have used 'magic' stones for a wide variety of purposes over the years and, ever since Columba's day, the island has been besieged by visitors who either wanted to take its stones away as souvenirs and talismans, or wanted to bury their dead beneath them. Kings, Lords of the Isles, and commoners all wanted to park their corpses half-way to heaven, their souls able to hitch a ride the rest of the way with Columba. It became a cumulative excercise, for the locals would lever up the ancient grave-slabs and plant the remains of their loved ones on top of whatever bones already lay crumbling – easier than digging a new grave in the thin earth. During this century both the unfortunate 'Lost Ladye' Norah Fornario, immortalised in Helen B. Cruikshank's poem, and Marjory Kennedy-Fraser, famous for collecting Songs of the Hebrides, were buried there. The Reilig Odhrain (Oran's burial ground), is rich with potash from crematoria and is still used by the islanders.

Not so long ago, a stone turned up on Iona. Mairi MacArthur of the New Iona Press, whose books draw on oral as well as documented sources for the island's history, is descended from generations of Iona people. Her family worked Clachanach (Stony Field) north of the Abbey. The wheel of her great-grandfather's cart kept striking an obstinate stone close to the spot known as Cladh nan Diseart (burial place of the hermit), down by the eastern shore. One day he set to, to dig up the offending item. It turned out to be a flattish stone with a little cross incised on one face. Today it is the only one kept locked in an iron cage in the Abbey Museum. It is labelled 'St Columba's Pillow'.

New stones turn up on the island as fast as others disappear. High on the shoulder of Dun I lies one apparently carved with hoof-prints; nobody now knows what it signified. The

Abbey's marble altar was gradually whittled away by folk wanting antidotes or souvenirs till, thanks to their attentions, by the 1770s the altar had been reduced to fragments. Martin Martin, a traveller to Iona in 1695, wrote of 'the Black Stone on which any oath sworn was most solemnly binding', also said to be an antidote to disease in either man or beast, forever being used to cure 'the bloody flux'. Boswell said it was partly buried in the soil near the Abbey, but it has now vanished. MacArthur reminds us that the description *dubh* (black) does not necessarily refer to the colour. It also means the possession of dark magic powers. The translucent green serpentine rock commonly found at the bay where Columba landed is said to confer immunity from drowning on its owner. Every visitor to the island wants an Iona stone as souvenir, a talisman, a charm.

Entrepreneurial local children, always short of a penny or two, took to supplying this demand, selling pebbles and shells to the tourists. Martin recorded a local belief in another Stone on Iona which, 'if an arm was stretched over it three times in the name of the Trinity, would grant skill in the steering of a ship'. This has gone too, as have the stone fonts that were said once to have stood between the cathedral and the nunnery which, 'if emptied of rainwater by a virgin, would ensure a fair wind for sailing'.

MacArthur mentions the Clachan Brath or Judgement Day Stones, three globes of white marble which were supposed to be turned sunwise in their stone basin by every passer-by. 'When the basin was finally worn through, this would herald the end of the world' – echoing the pre-Christian ritual of dedication to the sun. These too had gone from Iona by 1819.

From 1792 till 1840 the local schoolmaster, Allan Maclean, acted as official guide on the island. Well-liked and respected by both islanders and visitors, he took enormous interest in local history and could communicate in English. 'So strong was his feeling for his darling ruins that he could not speak with any patience of an Englishman having clandestinely carried off one of the figures that graced a tomb.' In 1819 a bunch of sailors was seen to vandalise one of the tombs, egged on by one of their officers for a double ration of grog.

Robert Chambers, a visitor to the island in 1840, repeated two mistaken myths about Iona often quoted as fact: 'Here are deposited the remains of forty-eight kings' and 'there were, at one time, three hundred and sixty stone crosses in different parts of Iona'. But he was clearly angry that the Abbey ruins were quarried 'to build cottages and make enclosures, the stolen materials of which betray themselves every where.' He wrote of

> the degree of culpable carelessness in protecting the religious buildings observable since that period, have operated in wasting and carrying off nearly every relic ... Among the most conspicuous of those remaining is ... a truly rich and elegant piece of sculpture ... the letters composing the inscription were originally run full of melted silver ... too great a temptation to escape the rude hands of the populace.

The nineteenth-century folklorist Alexander Carmichael found a *leag gruagach* or flat milk stone, named the Clach a'Bhainne, still in use a few yards from the site of today's telephone boxes, over which the girls poured a little milk on their way home from the cows in the pasture, to placate the *gruagach* – the spirit which guards cattle.

In order to assess the feelings Columba engendered in his people and the reverence with which his possessions were therefore regarded, we will follow him to his grave. He had based himself on Iona for thirty-four years. Adamnan writes: 'The old man, worn out with age, went in a cart one day in the month of May ... to visit some of the brethren who were at work ... on the western side of the island'. There he told his monks he would be quite glad to die, but didn't want to cause them sorrow at such a happy time of year, so would wait awhile. 'Then ... he turned his face to the east, still seated as he was in his chariot, and blessed the island with its inhabitants.' Later that year, at harvest-time, the angel of death comes calling for him. Columba blesses the corn and says he's glad the people will have enough to eat that winter. On his way back to the monastery 'bowed down with old age' he stopped to rest. 'Behold, there came up to him a white pack-horse, the same that used, as a willing servant, to carry the milk-vessels from the cowshed to the monastery. It came up to the saint and, strange to say, laid its head on his bosom . . . and, knowing that its master was soon about to leave it, and that it would see him no more – began to utter plaintive cries, and like a human being, to shed copious tears.' Columba comforted the horse, and blessed it. After attending a service, he 'returned to his chamber, and spent the remainder of the night on his bed, where he had a bare flag for his couch, and for his pillow a stone, which stands to this day as a kind of monument beside his grave. . .As soon as the bell tolled midnight, he rose hastily, and went to the church; and running more quickly than the rest, he entered it alone, and knelt down in prayer beside the altar.' Diormit, following him,

> found the saint lying before the altar; and raising him up a little, he sat down beside him and laid his holy head on his bosom. Meanwhile the rest of the monks ran in hastily . . . and beholding their dying father, burst into lamentations . . . Diormit then raised the holy right hand of the saint, that he might bless his assembled monks. And the venerable father himself moved his hand at the same time, as well as he was able – that as he could not in words, while his soul was departing, he might at least, by the motion of his hand, be seen to bless his brethren. And having given them his holy benediction in this way, he immediately breathed his last . . .

And so we leave Columba, the man who poet Kenneth Macleod called 'King of Storms' for his alleged ability to quell the raging sea.

It is some time later that we begin to hear about relics, altar stones and the like. A cross was still in existence, in Adamnan's day, where the old horse had made its farewell. In 1904 the carefully buried skeleton of a horse was discovered near the Abbey, its remains to be examined in Edinburgh. Various aspects of the burial make it look likely that it dates from the sixth century, when nobody would have bothered to inter a horse unless there was something very special about it. There is still a fascination with Columba. Surely we can therefore understand those earlier Scots who so treasured his relics and his memory.

Iona annually attracts some 200,000 people from all over the world. Why do they come? What is it they hope to find? The answer is, a mixture of things. The Iona Community began earlier this century because Lord Macleod of Fuinary wanted to rediscover the simplicity of Columba's religion, and it draws others seeking peace of mind, or their own religious experience. Tourists come for souvenirs, photographs, or to experience the beautiful wild 'natural' environment. But most come because, 1400 years ago, St Columba dwelt there.

If any stones connected with Columba remain undetected beneath the Ionian sod or hidden by the green waves of its sea, it is perhaps as well. We seem to have a greed for the material relics of religions in which we no longer believe, as though they in themselves are capable of bringing us solace. Is this perhaps why we feel as we do about the Stone of Destiny? And is this why the individuals who were involved in the Westminster episode of the 1950s proudly sport their fragments of that Stone?

CHAPTER TEN

≈

DUNSTAFFNAGE

Iona fell victim to the Viking scourge. After this, Professor Cowan says, 'Kenneth Mac Alpin divided the relics of Columba, sent some of them to Kells and brought the others to Dunkeld, after he moved into Pictland as a result, we think, of Viking pressure.

'Iona didn't collapse. The old books used to say the monastery succumbed to Viking attacks – we now know that's not true, but the monks were very hard hit indeed in the first half of the ninth century, and although it's not documented we have to assume that the rest of the coast of Dalriada was too. It's a difficult place to get out of, in the sense that, if the Vikings are putting up all this pressure from the sea, then the natives – the Scotti – are pretty well hemmed in by the mountains, so they don't have much option but to move out. But we have no evidence of a stone being mentioned along with relics. Absence of any *evidence* is my problem, and so there are just as many difficulties in proving this as in disproving it.'

By the year 849, Columba's relics were split between Kells in Ireland, founded by an Iona abbot forty years before, and the newly established Dunkeld.

The connection of Dunstaffnage, near Oban, with the Stone of Destiny is confused but persistent, covering two quite separate periods of its existence. And there are those who believe it has never left the castle.

Dunstaffnage Castle squats on a knob of old red conglomerate which once boiled up from flat rocks between the Firth of Lorn and Loch Etive, Argyll. Eastward from the wall-walk, beyond the grey awkwardness of Connel Bridge,

79

Loch Etive stretches to the foot of Ben Cruachan. Northwards lie Lismore and Morvern, and westward squats the great bulk of Mull. Much remains of the original stronghold, built for the MacDougalls of Lorne in the thirteenth century, who entered it through a natural rock fissure. Nearby, hidden in the woods, is a ruined chapel built soon after. The 'dog tooth' decoration of its windows matches those at the nunnery on Iona and helps date it.

Robert the Bruce took Dunstaffnage from the MacDougalls of Lorne, and it belonged to Scottish royalty for some years. It seems probable that Bruce would know the whereabouts of the Stone, and what it looked like, because it had been in use during his lifetime. It was not his fault if, like so many valuable hoards hidden in times of danger, it was lost.

Writer Lorn MacIntyre, who grew up nearby, notes that Bruce, who normally demolished castles so they could no longer be used by the English to oppress Scots, for some reason spared Dunstaffnage. Could it be because it was a place of safe-keeping for the Stone? And if you want to hide a large stone, what better than to build it into your nine-feet-thick wall along with hundreds more like it?

In 1470 the castle was handed over to Colin, first Earl of Argyll, and its custody vested in his cousin, the Captain of Dunstaffnage. Today the twenty-second hereditary Captain, Michael Campbell, keeps his title by sleeping in the castle annually, on midsummer's night, and some of his family believe the Stone of Destiny is still hidden there.

Down the years an intense interest has been shown by historians in the area around Dunstaffnage. Its very name rewards scrutiny, 'Dun' being Celtic for 'hill-fortress' and thus an old word, 'Staffnage' being a corruption of the Norse *staf-an-ness* ('promontory of the staff'), therefore a word dating from the eighth century Viking invasions. And it has had ecclesiastical associations since Columba's day. Historians are certain the dun originally had a fully Celtic name, and that the castle may be built on the mysterious lost fortress of Dun Monaidh, on record as a seventh century seat of the kings of Dalriada, like Dunadd. If that is true, then association with the Stone of Destiny is possible.

Two Celtic missionaries are connected with the area: an Irishman, Maelrubha, who towards the end of the seventh century founded a church at or near Dunstaffnage, referred to in a sixteenth century document as Kilmorrie, or Cladh Morrie (church/burial ground of Maelrubha). It was normal to plant your preaching station close to the fortified residence of the local chief, and usual to build on the 'holy ground' of a previous church. Some say Maelrubha's was at Dunstaffnage, others prefer the 'Green Chapel' across the present Dalmally to Oban road. St Convall, or Conall, is connected with an area he called 'Evonium' by Thomas Dempster, a seventeenth century hagiographer, and his contemporary David Camerarius, who also used old sources, tells us St Conall was honoured by Aidan, King of Dalriada. His chapel may have been the one that existed on a flat-topped mound two miles south-east of Dunstaffnage, near Ardchonnel Farm. Clearly the area had strong links with the Celtic church and Ireland, as well as with royalty, and any revered relics from Iona are likely at least to have passed through such a holy place en route to Dunkeld.

Translators are responsible for quite a confusion of names around the Dunstaffnage area, and therefore about the possible whereabouts of any Stone of Destiny. Boece, writing his history in Latin, used 'Evonium' as an alternative name for Dunstaffnage, and this was rendered by his translator Bellenden: 'King Ewyne biggit ane castel nocht far fra *Berigon* . . . quilk wes callit eftir Dounstaffnage.'

Two miles northward across the mouth of Loch Etive, antiquarian R. Angus Smith was ploutering about the shore in 1870. What he found there led him to write that Dun Sniochan, a rocky mound by the sea below Ben Lora, may have been Beregonium. The requirements are all there: a local tradition that six kings once dwelt there, including Fergus and Fingal;

evidence of ancient building, plus the remains of a Columban church and burial ground. Might not Columba's relics have been kept here rather than at Dunstaffnage across the bay? And if so, might there not be items yet to be discovered – perhaps even the stones on which he slept?

Alternatively, Ewen de Ergadia, reputedly a vigorous and very handsome knight, great-grandson of the mighty Somerled, whose main stronghold was Dunstaffnage, might have preferred to keep them at the fortress of Cenel Loairn, on the site of which we now find the ruins of Dunollie Castle, along with his own inaugural Stone.

Tantalisingly, none of the accounts give an exact location for inauguration ceremonies. Bellenden writes: 'Fergus . . . wes crounit in the fatale chiar of merbil, quhilk he brocht with him . . . to stabill his realme in Albion . . . In this chiar all kingis of Scotland war ay crownit, quhil the time of King Robert Bruse' – but where?

In the writings of a sixteenth-century character, John Monipennie, we first find mention of 'The most ancient castle of Dunstaffnage, in which were the kings of Scotland in old times crowned, where also the Marble fatall Chayre remayned more then one thousand yaeres'.

Late in the eighteenth century two tourists separately visited Dunstaffnage. One was told nothing about the Stone of Destiny, the other was given the full story. On 6th June 1760, Bishop Pococke heard the history of the castle minus any mention of the Stone, while twelve years later Thomas Pennant was being regaled with tales about the marble chair. Perhaps Pennant's informant was the fourteenth Captain, Donald Campbell, or someone who knew of a local tradition, or had access to a now-lost source of knowledge.

Nigel Tranter sews up the gaping seams of known history in his attempt to understand *why* the people of the past behaved as they did. In Tranter's novel *Kenneth*, long before he is king, Mac Alpin explores Dunstaffnage with the beautiful Princess Eithne. Lighting torches of bog pine, they investigate an underground earth-house. There they find the Stone, 'almost black, with its hollows and carvings picked out in the light of the flickering flames ... smooth, almost like marble.' As they leave, Eithne hears a strange rushing sound. It is the giant waterfall under the sea, written about by Ossian in 'Songs of Deirdre and the Sons of Uisneach', known as the Falls of Lora. One tradition says the Stone is hidden near a great waterfall, and the Falls of Lora must be one of the most powerful in Scotland, with the entire weight of Loch Etive behind it. Tranter has Mac Alpin taking the Stone to Iona, before returning it to Dunstaffnage, and going on to Dunadd to confirm his kingship while Eithne gives birth to their son. Whether Dunstaffnage, Dun Sniochan, Dunollie, or somewhere yet undiscovered was in fact once the lost city of Beregonium, the long local tradition that the Stone lies somewhere near Dunstaffnage is worth remembering, if we want to find the grain of fact necessary for its longevity.

≈

CHAPTER ELEVEN

SCOTLAND UNITED

W hichever of the legends about the origins of the Stone bears the truth, by the ninth century it had appeared in central Scotland, in what is now Perthshire.

Professor Duncan lists the peoples living north of Hadrian's Wall at that time: the Scotti in the west; Picts – believed to have been the aboriginal race – in the north, middle and east; Britons to the south. Round the coastline Vikings raped and pillaged, plundering rich pickings of meat, gold and jewels everywhere, especially from monasteries such as Iona. Not till much later did the Norse come to settle and bring new skills to northern Britain, or Alba as it became known.

While Scots wrote Ogham, Picts communicated in comic-strip, though they also appear to have had a script. Their earliest stones depicted animals, birds and fish along with symbols – Z rods, crescents and circles – and their later stones show the Christian cross along with these symbols. Finally they were using complete biblical iconography to show, for instance, Daniel and the lions. It is now thought that some Pictish designs were done in colour, likely because of the Picts' proven artistry and their noted love of brightly dyed clothing.

However all was not peace and beauty. The peoples of Alba were an aggressive lot. As the population increased, groups began to amalgamate both for defence and for acts of predation. Since about 600 they had probably been governed by a main king, with under-kings in certain areas. Constantine (789–820), listed in the Duan of Alban – the oldest known royal genealogy of Scotland – was one of the last Pictish kings. His brother Oengus is thought to have been the inspiration behind the Boar carving at Dunadd, and his nephew Eoghanan was killed in battle in 839. Kenneth Mac Alpin became King of the Scots in Dalriada in the middle of the ninth century, when old Alpin his father was killed in battle. He had a Pictish name, Cinead, and a Scottish granny descended from Fergus of Dalriada – and he somehow managed to become king of everyone in Alba by about 847, whether by inheritance or trickery we cannot yet tell. The story goes that Mac Alpin invited all the Pictish leaders to come to a grand banquet at Scone. The wine flowed freely and a great ceilidh was going on, with singing and dancing to take their minds off their troubles. Suddenly the benches gave way. Leading Picts were tumbled into a deep pit, and every one of them beheaded in a highly undemocratic, if effective, coup.

Mac Alpin lived in a period of violence and change throughout Europe, less than a century after Charlemagne. The Danes had just sacked London and were wreaking havoc throughout

Detail from Sueno's Stone

85

England, which wasn't unified for another fifty years. Kenneth Mac Alpin is the first important figure of Scottish history about whom a reasonable amount is known. He did move his centre of administration and his capital from Dunadd in Dalriada (Argyll) to Perthshire, though we can only speculate on his reasons for so doing. Perhaps it was in order to govern his enlarged kingdom according to Irish/Scottish custom, from its geographical centre, maybe for reasons of diplomacy – for Scone had been the sacred centre of Pictland.

Constantine had enlarged the Culdees' wattle church of nearby Dunkeld into a monastery, normal procedure when a conquering king wanted to confirm and sanctify his power over an area. At the point where legend leaches into known history around the mid-ninth century, MacAlpin had the remains of St Columba transported in the Monymusk Reliquary to Dunkeld. In placing such a venerated Scots symbol in a

Monymusk Reliquary, side.

Monymusk Reliquary, end. ? Eighth century.

Irish motifs on the Monymusk Reliquary. (Victorian Engraving. Reproduced by permission of the Museum of Antiquities, Edinburgh)

Pictish shrine, he showed psychological insight. Scots were now firmly planted, both symbolically and physically, in the seat of government, and their most important symbol was a stone of inauguration.

The Monymusk Reliquary is a small container, yet it was afterward regarded in its own right as a sacred object, having its own dewar (caretaker). It was carried before the Scottish army at Bannockburn as a talisman, and it can still be seen in Edinburgh, where it is carefully preserved in the National Museum of Scotland. While the Monymusk Reliquary would not have been difficult to transport overland in the mid-ninth century, the Stone of Destiny would have been a much trickier proposition. Heavy objects can be slung on poles, can be transported over bog, sod and rock on sleds. Boats and rafts can be pulled up lochs and rivers. But moving the Stone of Destiny could not have been an easy task, given the topography of Alba. Travellers then would have had to follow the same lochs, rivers and passes as the main road system does today, only instead of denuded hillsides and the hazards of tour buses, they would have faced bears, boars and wolves, undrained swamp and stands of virgin forest.

Somehow the procession wound its way along the shores of Loch Etive, up the River Awe through the Pass of Brander into the dark deeps beneath Cruachan, along the northern shores, past the headland on which Kilchurn Castle now stands, to Dalmally. From Dunadd the route followed the River Add, through Auchindrain to the coast at Pennymore. Then north-east via Inveraray, up Glen Aray, Glen Shira or Glen Fyne to meet the west-east paths. Onward through Glen Lochy, Crianlarich, and down the Dochart to Loch Tay. An easier passage then, below the majesty of Ben Lawers to where the black Tay pours eastward wide and strong through its strath, past Kenmore, Dull, Aberfeldy, round the wide sweep at Grandtully and southward to Dunkeld.

Tranter envisages a mile-long cavalcade, not unlike those parades of holy relics we see in Europe. The procession sets off from Dunstaffnage one morning in mid-April, a particularly beautiful time in Scotland, with the first greening of the countryside after winter. Even when it's raining, the air of Argyll fills with the erotic perfumes of spring; its woodlands pink and white with anemones, the burn-sides curly with unfurling ferns, and everywhere the lushness of bluebells coming on. Through this countryside, Mac Alpin's people carry their sacred Stone of Destiny towards Strathfillan and Loch Earn and then to Forteviot. Nobles and notables greet the procession at Forteviot. There is much feasting and fun till the great day of Mac Alpin's coronation, when they ride to Scone dressed in their finest clothes, accompanied by musicians. The ceremony is held in the open, by a small mound near the church. Psalms are sung and Kenneth is elected king through a series of long speeches by the ri, the lesser kings of Alba. He calls on a sennachie, or bard, to pronounce his identity and genealogy, which would have been sung or chanted from memory.

In reality, Mac Alpin did take charge, fighting off the Norsemen, attempting to control the Lothians in spite of its population of Angles, and drawing up the first Code of Laws for Scotland. He ruled over the areas we now name Perthshire, Fife, Stirlingshire, Dumbartonshire and much of Argyll. He and Eithne had a large family. Either his son or a brother, Gregor, became the founder of Clan MacGregor, which later became a threat to the unity of the Scottish throne.

Meanwhile, with the dusty remnants of Columba buried under the chancel of his new stone church at Dunkeld, he built himself a palace at St Andrews and a fine timber-framed, thatched hall at Forteviot. Eithne had a house at Forfar too. Mac Alpin reigned firmly and effectively over a good proportion of the Scottish people for sixteen years. Where exactly did he plant the Stone of Destiny to keep him lucky? Professor Cowan suggests Dunkeld, or possibly St Andrews.

There were the fringes of course – Mac Alpin never quite managed to persuade either the Angles of Lothian or the

Britons of Strathclyde to join him, and quelling the Vikings took even longer.

Not yet sixty, Mac Alpin died at Forteviot, the ancestor of all Scottish royalty, where today acres of fascinating lumps and bumps lie almost untouched beneath the pasture, waiting to reveal their treasures. He is supposed to have been buried at Iona, although the sheer impracticality of this gives rise to doubt. For some reason Mac Alpin was known as 'Rex Pictorum' – not till his grandson Donald does the title 'King of Alba' appear.

But by the end of the ninth century Alba was a nation. Most people were Christian. They were governed by a single king who was inaugurated upon a stone, which may have conferred nationhood on the Scottish people, but which did nothing to protect the long string of kings, some good, some bad, chosen from a kind of familial short-leet for their good qualities, some mere infants, who were to follow Mac Alpin, and whose normal form of death was murder most foul.

CHAPTER TWELVE

≈

WHO OWNS SCOTLAND?

With the Stone of Destiny firmly planted in Scone, in use for the inauguration of the kings of Scotland until 1292, perhaps it is time to pause for a brief overview of some of the tortuous history of Scotland, in an effort to understand where Edward I of England ever got the idea that Scotland belonged to him. For it was his anger, against the people he saw as his recalcitrant vassal Scots, that caused him to wreak havoc up and down their country, and finally to wrest from them the symbol of their kingship, their Stone.

Throughout the centuries, English kings attempted, by tricks, treaties, weddings and wars, to annex Scotland.

The British Isles were first governed by several minor kings, the southern English beginning to unify under Aelfred the Great of Wessex around the end of the ninth century. The push northward then began. His grandson Athelstan captured York and became king of all England. Naturally Athelstan and his subjects expected the northern thrust to continue.

Meanwhile in Scotland Constantine II, inaugurated on the Stone of Destiny in 900, wanted Lothian and Northumbria – good agricultural land – so much that he was prepared to do almost anything to acquire it from Athelstan. He started a trend that was to bedevil Scotland for centuries, and had to pay for his new territory by literally grovelling at the English king's feet.

His brother, Malcolm I, swore to be 'the English king's fellow worker both by sea and land' in return for Cumbria. In 975 Kenneth II rowed up the River Dee at Chester, with King Edgar of Wessex at the prow demonstrating his suzerainty, in return for Lothian and the re-issue of Cumbria.

The practice of Scottish kings paying lip-service to the superiority of English kings in return for border country continued. Malcolm II fixed the border at the River Tweed. But his successor Duncan I so misgoverned Scotland that the people replaced him with the Mormaer (lord) of Moray, Macbeth. Macbeth and his wife Gruoch ruled unusually well for seventeen years, persuading the Scottish populace into some semblance of law and order.

Peace did not last. Son of the dead Duncan, Malcolm Ceanmor grew up in England. He did not overcome Macbeth single-handed – he paid lowland and English lords for their help, with land. This habit of paying for services with good land was repeated by later kings.

But the English had not bargained for their own total defeat by the Normans. After 1066 it took William the Conqueror five years to reach Scotland, where Malcolm was forced to acknowledge him as overlord of somewhere, though no one was very clear where. After Malcolm and his saintly Queen Margaret passed into history, one king after another bounced on and off the Stone of Destiny, often murdering each other for the privilege. Lowland Scotland was made feudal quite successfully thanks to kings such as David I (r. 1124–1153).

The feudal system was like a pyramid, with God on top giving the king all the land of his kingdom and the Divine Right to rule it. The king leased parcels of land to his lords in return for goods and services, especially the provision of fighting men. The lords parcelled out theirs, and so on down the line. The king, being overall landowner, could re-negotiate these arrangements at will, redistributing land to people he liked, or to whom he owed a favour. It worked. The king commanded a centrally organised government, and had plenty of power over his nobles, who would think twice before rebelling. He had at his command an instant army without having to pay for its keep in times of peace, and he could call up local drafts whenever invasion threatened or internal troubles arose. William the Conqueror never actually conquered Scotland, either lowland or highland, and by no stretch of the imagination did God ever donate to him any of the land north of the Tweed-Solway line.

The kinship system of Scotland was quite different from feudalism. A clan chieftain's relationship with his people was supposed to be paternal, rather than one of a god to his supplicants. The land was common, to be grazed, farmed and roamed over more or less freely till the eighteenth century, the days of Enclosure, and the Clearances, when many a trusted clan chieftain would renege on his responsibilities. No chief was going to waste perfectly good fighting men on the king's military service unless he agreed with the reason for the war in the first place.

Accident-prone William (1165-1214), was romanticised by later generations as the 'Lion' because of Fordoun's description of him as '*leo justitiae*'. The red lion rampant on the yellow battle flag is supposed to derive from his day. But when he tried to take Alnwick Castle in Northumbria, his horse fell on him, neatly trapping him for capture. Delivered in chains to Henry II, he was forced to buy his freedom with homage. Behind Henry's back he continued to plot with France. Captured again, he found himself in Falaise, in fetters. This time, he bought his freedom by swearing away the whole of Scotland, giving the Scottish Church to the English, donating his border strongholds, lending his brother David as a hostage, and taking the bill home. In an effort to get God on his side he founded a new Abbey at Abroath.

Richard I came to the English throne full of missionary zeal, wanting cash for the Crusades. He sold Scotland back to the Scots for 10,000 silver marks – about a tenth of the total coinage in circulation in Scotland at the time. That freedom was genuinely bought. Scots then suffered a series of child kings and regencies. Henry III of England thought he'd found an easy number in Alexander III, crowned on the Stone of Destiny aged eight, and made him marry his daughter Margaret. She wore a robe of violet brocade with three small leopards embroidered on the front and back, and there was quite a party. Alexander duly knelt to Henry for lands he held in England but, though so young, evaded Henry's demand that he do homage and fealty for his kingdom of Scotland. Alexander said politely but diplomatically, 'I have come hither in peace . . . to be allied to you by marriage, and not to reply to you about so difficult a question. For I have not held deliberation concerning this with my chief men, as so difficult a matter demands.' Historians are still divided as to whether it was tact, appeasement or duplicity that made Alexander obey a call, in 1274, to the coronation of Edward I, as his vassal. Perhaps, under these circumstances, it is not so surprising that Edward I so strongly believed that Scotland belonged to him.

Bruce put England right, briefly, at Bannockburn in 1314, and the pope backed him up, saying he was king of Scots in his own right, and owed fealty to no one. Yet the kings who followed Bruce went on trying to give Scotland away, pawn it, sell it, with few exceptions. David II, possibly one of the best kings Scotland had, was captured by England and had to pay ransom. He kept hoping for an heir, to carry on the Bruce line, to free Scotland, but it was not to be. Plague then killed off many important people. 'Auld Blearie', King Robert II, crowned at Scone in March 1372, was a political survivor who may even have entered into treasonable negotiations with England.

The Church next gave Scotland a rough time. While Henry VIII of England was inventing divorce and espousing the Protestant cause to help him, Catholic Mary floated up the Forth to become Queen of Scots. Then suddenly Scots saw the light lit by John Knox. Armed with torches and Godly Truth, 'the rascal multitude' set out to purge Scotland of the excesses of complacent ecclesiastics, with such fanaticism that, once started, Knox couldn't stop them, tearing down churches and statues, burning books. By the time Cromwell's occupation was over in the seventeenth century, hardly a molecule of our documentation, our art, our culture, remained.

There are those who argue that the fundamentalist Presbyterianism which followed gave us our fabled work ethic, our honesty, and our hunger for learning. Maybe. But it also produced a meanness of spirit, a taste for punishment, a narrow parochialism, traits not far beneath the surface of many a Scots character, for hypocrisy lives and breathes in every glen and in every street in Scotland to this day.

The monarch who was to usher Scotland into final and binding union with England was a woman. Queen Anne, recognised by the Scottish Parliament in June 1702, only ever visited Scotland once, spending her seventeenth birthday in Edinburgh. Although she had eighteen children, all of whom predeceased her, and her health was so weakened by childhood smallpox and arthritis that she rushed about in a chariot like a gouty Boadicea, she did give Scotland her attention, and was personally present in the English Parliament whenever union was discussed.

It had been Malcolm Ceanmor who began the infiltration into Scotland of what has been called the 'English party', whereby Scottish lords could be bribed to promote English causes in Scotland. This process continued till Scotland finally succumbed through the Act of Union in 1707.

The disastrous Darien scheme, that misjudged attempt at colonialism, had bled Scottish coffers white, civil war was in the air, and Anne, along with many others, genuinely believed that union with England was the only solution. Relations between the two countries remained poor. England, fearing a Catholic Stewart succession allied to France, was not keen to take poverty-stricken Scotland on board: 'Whoever married a beggar cou'd only exspect a louse for a portion' went the saying.

Scots could see the risk of being swallowed by the larger state – 5 million English against 1 million Scots. In 1704 Scottish politicians were thinking seriously about re-establishing independence under a new monarch in spite of Anne's efforts, and they wanted nothing to do with the proposed Hanoverian succession. The main reason they failed was, as ever, that they could not agree among themselves.

The English, ambitious to establish themselves as a major military power in Europe, began to apply pressure, with the Alien Act of 1705, whereby Scots would be declared aliens if they refused to accept the Hanoverians. This meant all the property owned by Scots in England would be forfeit, and their rich trade with English colonies would be no more. On the other hand, in return for compliance there would be plenty of money. A disgusted Robert Burns accused Scotland of letting herself be 'bought and sold for English gold'.

Only a handful of men attended the Scottish parliament which agreed to the queen's commissioners being appointed to negotiate the union. Discussions only lasted from April 1706 to mid-July. In spite of 'roars of protest' when the terms were published, the Scottish Parliament voted in favour on 16th January 1707, putting themselves and their queen out of business at the dissolution signed by her on 28th April 1707 – 'ane end of ane auld song'. By the terms, theoretically England and Scotland became one country. Anne was Queen of Great Britain. The two parliaments were to be dissolved and a new one created.

Scotland had 45 seats in the Commons to England's 513 and 16 peers in the Lords to 190 English. While the ratio of populations was five to one, the ratio of members was more than ten to one in the Commons, and twelve to one in the Lords. There was no doubt who held power over whom. Soon an Act was passed which undermined the independence of the Scottish judiciary, and in 1708 the Scottish Privy Council was abolished, leaving Scotland with no effective administration.

Why had the Scots so meekly agreed to such unequal terms? Was it an act of far-seeing parliamentarians, or of desperation? Yet, in 1713 Scots were in Parliament attempting to undo the Union. Of course they stood no chance. Fortunately the

Scottish legal system, the church, and education were left untouched, and one positive result of the new stability was to be the Scottish Enlightenment.

In 1714 Queen Anne died, and the Hanoverians took over. There were fruitless riots. Bonnie Prince Charlie came, and went. For a hundred years Scotland got on with her own affairs until Sir Walter Scott and, through him, Queen Victoria, began to reawaken a romantic interest in her ruins.

Above: Kay Matheson. *Reproduced by permission of* The Herald.

Left: Wendy Wood. *Reproduced by permission of* The Herald.

Left: Rector John MacCormick in 1951. *Reproduced by permission of* The Herald.

Below: Left to right: Cllr Bertie Gray, Gavin Vernon, Ian Hamilton and Alan Stuart in 1951. *Reproduced by permission of* The Herald.

The Stone of Scone. *Reproduced by permisssion of Westminster Abbey.*

Dunadd Hillfort crouches like a great lion in *A' Mhoine Mhor. Reproduced by permission of Andrew Morris.*

Above: Early carved
stones at Whithorn.
*Reproduced by
permission of the
Whithorn Trust.*

Left: Stone carving at
Melrose Abbey.
*Reproduced by
permission of
Historic Scotland.*

The Footprint, Dunadd in 1965, before capping. *Reproduced by permission of Ronald W.B. Morris.*

Skeletons of Whithorn people who might have seen Robert the Bruce. *Reproduced by permission of the Whithorn Trust.*

Left: The Stone believed to have been St Columba's pillow lies in the Abbey Museum. *Reproduced by permission of Iona Abbey Museum.*

Below: Edward I used Norham Castle as a base. *Reproduced by permission of Andrew Morris.*

Above: The western Seas, from Dunollie, near Oban. *Reproduced by permission of Andrew Morris.*

Below: Dunstaffnage Castle. *Reproduced by permission of Andrew Morris.*

Robert the Bruce gazes over Bannockburn. His head was modelled by Charles Pilkington-Jackson from the skull discovered at Dunfermline Abbey. *Reproduced by permission of Andrew Morris.*

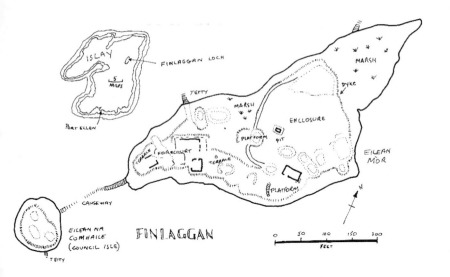

Finlaggan: Plan of Eilean Mòr (Large Island) and Eilean Comhaile (Council Isle).
Reproduced by permission of the Finlaggan Trust.

The fisherman may be standing on the secret causeway that lay just below water level in Loch Finlaggan, leading to Eilean Mòr. *Reproduced by permission of Andrew Morris.*

The Knights Templar take their stone into safe keeping. *Reproduced by permission of* The Herald.

Dunnsinnan means 'the fort of the nipple'. Macbeth's Castle is an ancient fort on its top. *Reproduced by permission of Andrew Morris.*

Dr Fiona Watson looks to the future as one of the new breed of Scottish historians. *Reproduced by permission of D.C.Thomson.*

Dr Hamish Henderson sings his freedom Come-All-Ye at Strichen, with a wee dram in his hand. *Reproduced by permission of Andrew Morris.*

7.am. Under cover of darkness the Stone is taken from Westminster Abbey. The congregaton feel bereaved. *Reproduced by permission of* The Scotsman.

Kay Matheson, hailed as a heroine by the crowds, sees her stone onto its new home in Edinburgh, watched by Alex Salmond. *Reproduced by permission of The Sunday Mail.*

Daniel in the Lions' Den shows the Christian side of the Guinevere Stone at Meigle Museum. *Reproduced by permission of the Meigle Museum.*

Below: I.O.U. Prince Andrew lends Secretary of State Michael Forsyth his stone. *Reproduced by permission of* The Sunday Post.

Stone Throne. *Reproduced by permission of* The Herald.

Scul?tor George Wyllie wonders what Scotland's Destiny will be. *Reproduced by permission of Andrew Morris.*

CHAPTER THIRTEEN

≈

ENGLAND'S EDWARD AND THE CELTIC FRINGES

'How I rocked Scots on Stones Tour of 1296' sings a headline on 16th November 1996. Cheery Jeremy Hodges of the *Express* goes on to suggest what 'old Longshanks' might have to say about his 'date with Destiny' from 'beyond the grave', leavened with mirth about the 'half-baked Stone of Scone', and incorporating many a home truth.

Since much of the mystery about the whereabouts of the Stone of Destiny depends on the thoughts and actions of Edward I, it seems only fair to take a closer look at the English point of view. This may help us to assess the persistent tradition that the original Stone never went south of the border. So, was Edward Plantagenet anything more than a thirteenth-century thug?

At a time when kings had to be seen to be smiled upon by God – healthy, rich and powerful, the young Prince Edward looked like everyone's idea of a medieval hero. Born in the year 1239, he grew to an immensely strong six foot two inches in height, he could leap fully armed into the saddle without stirrups, and he was a bonny fighter. He managed to overthrow his father's imprisoner Simon de Montfort, and in 1272 had himself crowned King of England. He was thirty five, full of new ideas, and deeply in love with his queen, Eleanor.

But what was Edward really like? The Song of Lewes compared him to the lion: brave, proud and fierce, but also to the leopard: inconsistent and unreliable, prone to giving promises when cornered, then reneging on them as soon as the opportunity arose. The chronicler Matthew Paris enthusiastically noted vices, such as Edward and his bodyguard mutilating a peasant they encountered on the road, simply for the fun of torturing him.

For a time Edward improved with age, becoming conscientious and self-disciplined. Frugal eating and drinking habits kept him slim and fit. His manner was grave, courteous and frank and he made a good impression on his subjects. He was a committed Christian, going on the required Crusade to Jerusalem, and he insisted on sharing his army's hardships on campaigns till he was over sixty.

He lived in interesting times. With the Crusades ended, Marco Polo wandering between Europe and China, and the Vikings gone, England could concentrate on the wool business. Her merchants grew wealthy, and universities were founded. So greedy eyes were cast on Edward's country.

He took over government at a time of great change. Simon de Montfort, in order to gain people's co-operation, had attempted to govern with their consent and Edward liked this idea, opining that a country should function like a human body in which all the parts worked together. From time to time Edward held the talking shops in Westminster Hall that came to be known as parliaments. These were to offer advice, not to take decisions. Here, wrote a contemporary 'justice is done to everyone according to his deserts'. Edward is credited with important developments in English law, and England's experience of his reign was of innovation and justice, firm government, and the beginnings of democratic consultation. His dream was to bring all of Britain under the rule of the Plantagenet dynasty. This, of course, was a perfectly sensible idea. The islands are not large, and would surely benefit from co-operation. Why waste energy on strife? Why risk the possibility of a disaffected section inviting in your enemies, such as the Norsemen or the French, by the back door?

While Edward was busy bringing law and order to England, the Celtic fringes were in constant turmoil. First he made an abortive attempt to subdue Ireland, whose seaway protected her. Next an opportunity arose for him to tackle Wales. The Welsh were aliens, with their Celtic language and laws, hidden beyond the mountains of Snowdonia. The powerful and charismatic Llywelyn, who had strong-armed most of the north-west of his country into some sort of unity, must be quelled, for he had 'missed' Edward's coronation. Failure to pay homage signalled, in feudal terms, Llywelyn's intention neither to obey Edward nor to support his wars.

It took Edward five years to annexe Wales, starving Llywelyn into defeat. The Welsh effectively collapsed, and soon found their country encircled with new castlefuls of Edward's soldiers. By incarcerating their little Princess Gwenllian in an English convent for the rest of her life, he extinguished the blood-line of the Welsh royal family forever. To emphasise his triumph Edward gave the title of Prince of Wales to a baby, his own son. His final act was to abstract the Stigmata, special treasures and relics of Wales, and parade them in mockery throughout other parts of Britain.

Edward had subdued Wales, but what of Scotland? He had sworn to take the whole of Britain. And his motto was 'I keep my promise'.

Scotland was a more daunting proposition. For centuries it had had its own line of royal kings, with all that implied in a feudal ruler's mind. No mere chieftain was in charge. Geographically and ethnically the country was divided: north of the Tay lived wandering herdsmen with their own language and customs, and wild tribes or clans who were to continue warring with one another quite happily for another four hundred years, unaffected by continental customs such as feudalism. But the rolling hills and lowlands south of the Forth-Clyde line were farmed by families descended from sixth century English settlers and Normans, their feudal system and ways of life not unlike those in England, and many great families – the Balliols and the Bruces for example – held land in both countries and so had no interest in war. Up to that time, while there were persistent territorial squabbles in the border area, there was little deep-seated antagonism between the two countries.

The thirteenth century had been particularly peaceful, helped by two dynastic marriages. Edward's aunt Joan wed Alexander II King of Scots, and his sister Margaret was Alexander III's first queen. But when Margaret died and was replaced by a Frenchwoman, Yolande of Dreux, in 1285, Edward saw Scotland drawing dangerously close to its old ally France.

Alexander III died tragically on 18th March 1286, galloping homeward from Edinburgh to Fife in rough weather after a party. Next morning he was found on the shore below Kinghorn cliffs, dead. The fourteenth-century poet and scholar John Barbour expressed the feelings of Scots at that time:

> Sen Alexander our king wes deid
> That Scotland left in luve and lee,
> Away wes sonse of aill and breid,
> Of wine and wax, of gamin and glee.
> The gold wes changit all in leid,
> The frute failyeit on everilk tree,
> Christ succour Scotland and remeid
> That stad is in perplexitie.

Possibly the temptation to subjugate Scotland was simply too great for Edward when, on that stormy March night, opportunity once again favoured him. There was a brief lull while the Scots waited to see if Yolande would produce a posthumous heir. None appeared. Edward, still the good modern thinker full of the best intentions, proposed a marriage between his heir and Alexander's little grand-daughter, the Maid of Norway, at the Treaty of Birgham. When she died, there was no one left to offer.

In an apparent effort to keep Scotland from tearing itself apart, Edward went north to advise on how the rival claims to their throne should be resolved. A ruler had to be found. At that time no form of government except feudalism existed.

It was essential to have a lord-superior at the top of the social and economic pyramid – otherwise the whole edifice, which depended on homage and fealty, would collapse. Edward did genuinely regard himself as overlord of Scotland and, as we have seen, there were good historical reasons for this. He even reinforced it by commissioning research in the monastic chronicles.

The year 1290 was a particularly dreadful one for the fifty-two year-old Edward. His beloved Eleanor suddenly died. Her untimely death had a terrible effect on his personality, turning him into an embittered and savage man. Put out by the failure of his plan to annexe Scotland at a time when he needed to concentrate on foreign issues, exasperated by the persistence of the Scottish problem, he travelled up to Norham on the River Tweed in May the following year to hold a Great Council. There, he persuaded the Scots to recognise his rights of overlordship at least during the hearings and discussions about which of the thirteen claimants to the throne would win. The possibility of gaining control of the whole of Britain must have seemed very real to Edward then.

Professor Duncan writes: 'There is no doubt that Edward's court tried to hear fairly the various claims put forward', and he appears to have gone to a great deal of trouble to listen to advice from learned people, churchmen and foreign lawyers. There was even a record of all the proceedings of The Great Cause, as the hearings came to be called, made by a public notary. Yet, while he appeared to be acting so impartially as both judge and jury at Norham, he ordered his fleet north, to lurk off Holy Island (Lindisfarne) ready to blockade the Scottish ports. He summoned his army from the north of England, and his treasurer suddenly started being difficult about debts owed to the crown. In the end, Edward stated baldly that he was overlord of Scotland, challenged the Scots to disprove it if they could, and took over ownership of the royal castles. For reasons of common sense he chose John Balliol – a man who, as an English baron, owed allegiance to him, but who was also genuinely of royal Scots descent. Balliol was to be king only if he would pay homage to Edward as overlord of Scotland.

Fordun describes the day, 17th November, when John Balliol was proclaimed king: 'The Earl of Gloucester, holding Robert the Bruce by the hand, in the sight of all, spoke thus to the king: "Recollect O King what kind of judgement thou hast given today and know that thou must be judged at the last", and straightaway at the Earl's bidding the aforesaid Robert Bruce withdrew, nor did he ever tender homage or fealty to John of Balliol.'

In Newcastle, Balliol knelt before Edward, accepting him as Lord Paramount both personally and for Scotland, after his coronation on St Andrew's Day, 30 November 1292, the last recorded inauguration of a Scottish king on the Stone of Destiny.

According to feudal theory, the relationship between England and Scotland should now have been of mutual benefit, Edward's overlordship implying not only submission to him by the Scottish people, but also his responsibility for their protection.

Balliol's press has traditionally been bad. Only his blood was Scottish. His life experience, lands and loves had all been in France and England. Lynch cites 'dispensation of justice on an unusual scale ... and consultation with the political community in parliament as well as council' as features of his reign. He may not have been such a bad man. As we have seen, Edward proceeded to turn him into a figure of ridicule. 'Toom Tabard' (empty coat), as Balliol came to be known, was a glove-puppet to Edward's hand in Scottish affairs and Edward had him running up and down to London like a lackey, on idiotic whims. It was when, eventually, Balliol lost patience and rebelled against him that Edward lost the remnants of his humanity. With quiet courage better suited to a Shakespearian hero than his weak image suggests, Balliol made an alliance with Philip IV of France, roundly accused Edward of having 'caused harm beyond measure to the liberties of ourselves and our kingdom', and renounced his fealty and homage 'which, be it said, were extorted by extreme coercion on your part'. This is what brought Edward raging north.

Scotland, his vassal state, was to be brought to heel. In 1296 the might of the English army, with its deadly longbows, was marched north to quell the country for once and for all, pausing only to make an example of the people at Berwick. The English sacked the prosperous little town and put 17,000 people to death, leaving their bodies to rot as a threat to any other would-be rebels north of the border. Thus began a chapter of unsurpassed violence in Scottish history that would go down to posterity as the Wars of Independence, and which were to last for almost two hundred years. While the bodies were still hanging from the windows, stinking in the gutters, Edward summoned the Scottish nobility to the town to sign what came to be known as the 'Ragman Rolls': 1,500 were forced, in that unforgettable atmosphere, to acknowledge his 'superiority'. Perhaps one understands why Balliol might have preferred civilised alliance with France to servitude as this tyrant's vassal. Weeks later the dead were shovelled into pits in order to repopulate the town with English incomers. Striking north, Edward took town after town: Dunbar, Stirling, Perth, then Brechin. At Montrose he had John Balliol dragged before him in chains. A great seal had been struck for the Guardians. Edward had it publicly smashed. His recorded words were: 'A man does good business when he rids himself of a turd.'

Edward reached Aberdeen a week later. All Scotland knew of his presence, his purpose, and his intention to take the Stone of Destiny. Averaging about twelve miles a day, he was across the Spey by Tuesday 24th July, turning south to reach Brechin by Saturday 5th August. The Abbot of Aberbrothock had been preaching subversive propaganda to his flock – 'there was but women and no men in England'. The churchmen of Scotland were not afraid of Edward.

By Wednesday 8th August 1296 Edward I was at St John's of Perth. Between the 5th and the 8th a stone was wrenched from Scone Abbey by Edward's men, a stone reputed to be the 'Palladium of Scotland', on which Balliol and all the Scottish kings before him had been crowned.

'*Apud Monasterium de Scone positus erat lapis pergrandis in ecclesia Dei, juxta magnum altare, concavus quidem ad modum rotundae cathedrae confectus, in quo futur reges loc quasi coronationis ponebantur exmore* ... (at Scone monastery was an unusually large stone in God's church, beside the high altar, concave like a round decorated chair in which kings would be crowned)', and at Edinburgh Castle in 1296 arrived '*una petra magna super quam Reges Scotieae solebant coronari*' (a large stone on which Scottish kings were crowned). It took his army some time to conquer their way to Edinburgh, but Edward finally arrived there in June. The Castle was well defended, but in the end it yielded and thereafter Edward's journey was little more than a triumphal march.

By the end of the year, his objectives apparently achieved, he returned to London, with John Balliol a prisoner bound for exile to France. Edward, now aged fifty-seven, ruled Scotland. From Edinburgh, he ordered the Scottish regalia taken to London, along with the Scottish emblem of kingship, the Stone from Scone, which was to be installed as a trophy of war at Westminster Abbey.

In Edward's wardrobe accounts for 1300 is a payment to Walter the Painter for the new chair '*in qua petra Scocie reponitur juxta altare ante feretrum Sancit Edwardi in Ecclesia Abbatie Westmonaster*' – in which the Scottish stone lies beside St Edward's Altar in Westminster Abbey.

In a 'parliament' Edward demanded obedience from the Scots as his subjects. Scotland was now an English colony.

Practically every book of English history that deals with this period mentions the legend of the 'Stone of Destiny'. By taking it away, Edward believed he had won a psychological victory that would be more effective than all his abortive wars. From now on he, Edward King of England, would crush the

Scots' ambitions of sovereignty, whenever he felt like it, and his heirs after him.

The Stone which arrived in London is described by the Royal Commission On Historical Monuments, London, as

> A quarry dressed block of coarse grained old red sandstone, measuring 26 1/2 inches by 16 1/2 inches by 11 inches thick. On it is a roughly incised cross, and an oblong indentation. It is fitted at the ends with iron staples, carrying rings which are so attached that a pole can easily be passed through them to facilitate carrying it. These cuttings are probably of the time of Edward I.

No expense was to be spared, and accordingly Edward ordered his goldsmith to make a fair bronze chair to contain it.

While the Abbey was closed to the public before the Coronation in 1953, the Ministry of Works took the time to examine it in detail. The workmanship and the actual materials used in the making of the chair were X-rayed, chemically analysed and minutely measured. No detail was overlooked. Lengthy and exhaustive reports were written by the Ministry of Works in 1953, notes were added, and the whole lot released into the public domain in 1996.

The coronation chair, which still stands in Westminster Abbey today, has been used in almost all English coronations since that of Edward II in 1307. We are told it was made by Walter of Durham in 1299 when he was aged about seventy. Walter had been the King's Sergeant Painter since 1270. According to the Wardrobe Accounts for 1300 it seems he was paid one hundred shillings for the Chair, 13s 4d for the carving and painting of two wooden leopards – kings of England during that period liked being shown with their feet resting on leopards, perhaps to model their throne on descriptions of King Solomon's which had 'two lions standing by the stays' – and £1 19s 7d for making a step and case for it. This evidence is currently disputed by scholars.

The earliest manuscript illustration showing the chair dates from the early fourteenth century and is owned by Corpus

Christi College, Cambridge. Its first appearance on a royal seal was the one engraved for Edward III in 1327 when the chair, being new and grand, receives more attention from the engraver than does the king.

But in spite of Edward Plantagenet's original order for a bronze chair, none of the research so far carried out by historians and scientists has revealed a single trace of bronze in the chair that Walter the Painter made so beautifully for him. Why not? Was Edward suddenly strapped for cash – or did he suddenly realise that the stone he had looted from Scone was not the Stone of Destiny? And if so, did he deliberately cover this up to save face?

Certainly he always appears to have treated the stone he brought from Scotland with respect. It is listed in several inventories of his most choice possessions. He was a most devout man, as well as a superstitious one; he carried sacred relics about on his person, such as his two pieces of the 'original' Calvary rock.

Aged sixty-eight, his health and strength exhausted, still obsessively convinced that he owned Scotland, and that the English army, God and his royal self would grind the Scottish people under his heel, this once respected monarch died in July 1307, demanding with his last gasp that his dead bones be carried into Scotland at the head of the English army, and that his tombstone would bear the epitaph Edward *Malleus Scottorum*, Hammer of the Scots.

≈

CHAPTER FOURTEEN

ROBERT THE BRUCE

For the first time in Scottish history, the people were moved to unite fully against a predator. The catalyst was the younger son of a Refrewshire laird, and his name was William Wallace. This large, unflinching and charismatic young man – who inspired the popular film *Braveheart* (1995) – appeared from nowhere in 1297 to galvanise anti-English feeling into organised revolt in Scotland.

Wallace himself had no ambition to sit on the Stone of Destiny. In fact, his aim was to restore John Balliol. After beating the English at Stirling Bridge, however, and raiding an English court at Scone in 1297, he allowed himself to be persuaded into becoming Guardian of Scotland. Only a year later he was defeated at Falkirk, outlawed, and forced to resign. He did so in favour of the joint guardianship of John Comyn and Robert the Bruce.

Through treachery, Wallace was caught and most cruelly executed according to Edward's command on 24th August 1305 in London. His mutilated body was distributed for display in Newcastle, Berwick, Stirling and Perth. But his exploits had caught the imagination and heart of Bruce, who decided that he must take on the cause of the nation into which he had been born.

Robert the Bruce was born on 11th July 1274 at Turnberry Castle in the idyllic south-west of Scotland. A lighthouse now blinks from its ruins, towards the nearby shore of Ulster. Bruce seems always to have had an affinity for this particular seaway and the Clyde estuary.

He first appears in history as a boy of twelve, witnessing a deed of Alexander Macdonald of Islay in the Paisley *registrum*.

We hear nothing more until he is eighteen, by which time it is clear that he was thoroughly educated, physically strong, well-trained in fighting skills, and a well-rounded, likeable individual. We know now that he was a stocky five feet six inches tall, and that his face had high cheekbones and a firm, square jaw.

The reasons Robert the Bruce became King of Scots have been thoroughly examined by scores of historians, poets, novelists and biographers down the ages. Every tourist to Scotland is dragged round dripping 'Bruce's' caves full of persevering spiders whose antecendents are supposed to have inspired the hero. However, in this publication we merely search his story for sufficient understanding to help keep us on the trail of the Stone of Destiny as it disappears once again into myth and legend.

There is no doubt that Bruce was an ambitious man, both for his family and for himself. His royal blood had come down the female line from Kenneth Mac Alpin. A lowland lord of Norman descent, Bruce's allegiances wavered while he was young, but by his early thirties his destiny was clear.

Edward I had marched off south about his business in 1296 flaunting his Stone, believing Scotland was conquered, and foolishly not bothering to consolidate his victory. Michael Lynch explains in his history *Scotland* (1991) how this failure was symptomatic of the failure of Edward's regime. For conquest and conciliation worked against each other; 'Forfeiture of lands in Scotland was a necessary device to compensate the English earls and captains, who remained mostly unpaid for their part in the Scottish campaigns; but a lasting reconciliation of disaffected Scottish nobles could be achieved only by a generous regrant of their lands.'

The two Guardians, Bruce and Comyn, had the most to gain. Never the best of friends, with Comyn supporting the Balliol cause, they had only been persuaded to work together with difficulty. In October came the news that Edward I was

ill. He might die. Bruce offered Comyn a deal: either you help
me onto the throne in return for my estates, or you give me
yours and I'll help you become king. Comyn opted for land,
and they exchanged signed indentures. Bruce was to be king.
Meanwhile Edward made a miraculous recovery.

According to the poet Barbour, in January 1306 Bruce and
Comyn were in London. Comyn gave his copy of their deal to
Edward, then raced homeward to Dumfries. Edward presented
the indenture to Bruce, demanding, 'Was it sealed by thee?'
According to A.A.H. Douglas's translation of Barbour, Bruce
replied:

> What simple fool I be!
> Not always is my seal with me.
> I have a man that bears the seal;
> And therefore, if it be your will,
> I ask respite that I may better
> Become acquainted with this letter.
>
> Tomorrow when you take your seat,
> And all your lords together meet,
> This letter shall I hither bear,
> That all your parliament may hear,
> And as security I pledge
> All lands that are my heritage . . .

Bruce hurries home to his lodgings and sends for his clerk:

> The Bruce bad fetch without delay
> Two sturdy horses to the door.
> He and the clerk, and no-one more,
> Leapt on the horses, all unseen;
> And day and night, with nought between
> They rode till in Lochmaben town
> The fifth day out they lighted down . . .
>
> It chanced that on that very day
> Within Dumfries, not far away,
> Sir John the Comyn made abode.
> The Bruce took horse and thither rode,
> Intent that he should speedily
> Avenge the other's treachery.

He lost no time and, hurrying on,
At Greyfriars he found Sir John
Beside the altar; lightly spoke,
And showed him, as it were a joke,
The signed indenture; then with a knife
Right on the spot he reft his life!

Doubt not, it was a great misdeed
Of holy altar to take no heed!
Thereby such hardship Bruce befell
That nee'er in story heard I tell
Of any man had such distress
Before he won to his success.

The thirty-one year-old Bruce was now in a most awkward situation. His decision was instant. He went straight to Glasgow to seek absolution from little old Bishop Wishart, who granted it, and sent word out around the country to that effect, telling the clergy to rally to Bruce as though to a sacred cause. In return Bruce promised to preserve and defend the Scottish Church. Feeling spiritually more at ease, he sent a formal demand to Edward I that he was to be recognised as King of Scots – and an urgent message to Bishop Lamberton to head for Scone without delay to crown him.

Bishop Lamberton sent his young protégé James Douglas ahead of him from Berwick, then under cover of darkness, rode direct to Scone. Barbour has Douglas meeting Bruce near Arickstone, and bowing low, saying he had come to do homage to him as rightful King and to share his fortunes, and Bruce knighting him there and then. The resulting friendship was to last throughout his life.

Tranter colours in the scene: he imagines 'a company of mounted instrumentalists and minstrels . . . banners fluttered by the score; gorgeously-caparisoned horses, heraldically-emblazoned litters, silks, satins, velvets and jewellery, dazzled the eye. Bruce himself wore a cloth-of-gold tabard, with the Lion of Scotland embroidered in red front and rear, picked out in rubies, and his queen was in royal purple velvet.'

It appears that ordinary people greeted Bruce and his

entourage with enthusiasm but, Tranter points out, they had 'little to lose, and at this stage not a great deal to contribute'. The landed nobles, knights and lairds, who alone could provide Bruce with armed forces, money and horses, held back, waiting to see, after ten years of warfare with England, what would happen. Bishop Wishart brought out the vestments of kingship he had hidden. It seems unlikely that the vestments were the only items to have been stashed away.

Tranter imagines his abbot, a small and cheery cleric of considerable age, leading Bruce and Lamberton down into the 'damp and dripping vaults', unlocking a door and, lifting his lantern high, triumphantly revealing the Stone of Destiny.

Details which have come down to us about the ceremony that took place at Scone that 25th March 1306 are tantalisingly brief. The vestments were placed around Bruce's shoulders. A simple circlet of gold was placed on his head. Lamberton anointed him with oil. Bruce did sit on what is described as the Coronation Chair. Did it contain – or was it indeed – the Stone of Destiny, brought out of hiding for the occasion by the spirited little abbot, who had, after all, been in charge when Edward's thugs arrived to steal it that August day in 1296?

The period between 30th November 1292, the date of Balliol's inauguration on the Stone, and 25th March 1306, is short – less than fourteen years passed between the two events. Bruce had attended the Balliol ceremony. If the Stone of Destiny was visible, he saw it. Dr Louise Yeoman of Scotland's National Library argues that, since Edward's 'battling bishop' Anthony de Beck of Durham not only saw Balliol crowned, but was also at the head of Edward's 'henchmen' when they came to plunder it from Scone, he would certainly have kicked up a fuss if it had been the wrong stone, and that only 'Mystic Megs' would think otherwise. But it doesn't take much magic to jalouse from the ancient seals that by the thirteenth century the Stone was being encased in an increasingly elaborate series of carved wooden seats. For inaugurations it was also draped with richly embroidered cloth and perhaps topped by a cushion. Would it not therefore have been rather difficult to scrutinise the Stone of Destiny in all its naked glory? Indeed, recent research is suggesting strongly that in fact Edward's men took the very chair which contained the Stone, perhaps to be a model for the proposed bronze throne, and later, when it was safely at Westminster, had it gilded in the English fashion. How easy, then, for an enterprising abbot to slot in a spoof stone for the occasion.

There is one unusual circumstance about Bruce's coronation. Noticeably absent was the young McDuff, Earl of Fife, traditionally the person charged with the duty of placing the crown on the head of the King of Scots. He was being held in England as a ward of Court. But Isabel, his nineteen-year-old sister, had heard about the coronation. She was married to the Earl of Buchan, an ally of Edward and kinsman of the dead Comyn. In spite of taking the Earl's best horse, and galloping towards Scone, she missed Bruce's coronation by a day.

Facing excommunication, Bruce was keen to have as many of the parts of the ceremony working for him as possible, so he arranged to go through a second coronation ceremony on Palm Sunday, forty-eight hours after the first, and for this, Isabel lifted the golden circlet and placed it on his brow, and he was truly King of Scots according to every tradition.

Members of the English court, who found it inconceivable that a woman could have a higher motive than sex for her actions, decided her dash to Bruce's side at Scone must mean she was his mistress. To thank her, Bruce's Queen Elizabeth took Isabel into her household as a lady-in-waiting. But when, later that year, they were captured along with Bruce's sister Mary at Tain, Edward I had them shut up in wooden cages like animals and exposed to public ridicule, Mary at Roxburgh Castle, and Isabel on the ramparts at Berwick. There they remained for *four years*. They barely survived. Meanwhile Bruce's daughter, the twelve-year-old Marjorie, was caged in the Tower of London, and Queen Elizabeth was shut away in a convent.

The pope not only excommunicated Bruce for his murder of the Comyn in Greyfriars Kirk, but placed an Interdict on Scotland. Bruce may have been crowned King of Scots, but he had yet to persuade many people to come round to him, and yet to regain their freedom for them. It took many years, during which he was hunted high and low, keeping on the move between Ireland, Carrick and Kyle, the Western Highlands and the islands. A brief respite only came when Edward I died.

But Bruce ruled wisely, and came to be well-loved by his people. Eventually, in March 1314, he heard that Edward II was coming north to 'save' Stirling Castle, garrisoned by the English, and under serious siege by Bruce's brother. At midsummer, the two armies met near the Bannock Burn, within view of the castle. Six thousand Scots miraculously defeated twenty thousand English. Such was the panic that Edward II lost his shield, his privy seal, and even his court poet, who was forced thereafter to compose victory verses for the Scots.

The Bannockburn victory finally established Bruce's authority, For his day he proved remarkably merciful. Prisoners were exchanged, and his long-suffering Queen Elizabeth, young Marjorie and Mary came home. Of Isabel there is no mention in the list of returnees, and it seems likely she died in the Carmelite nunnery to which she'd been sent. She can't have been more than twenty-seven.

Till then, Elizabeth did not have a relaxed life. Married to Bruce in her teens, fleeing through heather, struggling through ice and snow, imprisoned for years, she never knew if her husband was alive or dead. Bruce built a manor for them at Cardross, near Dumbarton on the Clyde. There they set out a garden, an aviary for their falcons and a slip for their boat. He could keep an eye on his navy at Dumbarton. Even in these propitious circumstances, they took six years to produce an heir. Bruce's problems were made immeasurably more difficult by the pope's sanctions. For the sake of the economy and his own immortal soul, Bruce needed to have them lifted.

Arbroath Abbey was his administrative centre, where Church affairs were headed by Lamberton, affairs of State by his Chancellor, the abbot of Arbroath, Bernard of Linton. The Declaration of Arbroath was probably written there under Bernard's supervision, perhaps by Alexander Kinninmonth, who was to take this persuasive document to the pope in Avignon. Sealed by eight earls and thirty-one barons, and in the name of the community of the realm, it was sent on its way in April 1320. Stressing the Scottish loyalty to the church, it tells how Scots dwelt in freedom and quietness till Edward I invaded their country in the guise of an ally. It describes his cruelties, and goes on -

> At length it pleased God ... to restore us to liberty ... by our most serene prince, King and Lord, Robert ... and the due and lawful consent and assent of all the people made him our King and prince. To him we are obliged and resolved to adhere in all things ... as being the person who has restored the people's safety, in defence of their liberties. But, after all, if this prince shall leave these principles he has so nobly pursued and consent that we of our Kingdom be subjected to the King of people of England, we will immediately endeavour to expel him as our enemy ... for so long as there shall be but one hundred of us remain alive we will never give consent to subject ourselves to the dominion of the English. For it is not glory, it is not riches, neither is it honour, but it is freedom alone that we fight and contend for, which no honest man will lose but with his life.

The writers reminded the pope that, since he himself would eventually be judged, would he please tell the King of England to be content with what he had. There is also a firm sentence about how the pope's conscience would be answerable for all the blood and 'loss of souls and other calamities' if he allowed the warring to go on. That this missive still has a reputation for stirring the souls of Scots was emphasised when film-star Sean Connery quoted from it in his famous party political broadcast for the SNP in November 1996.

It is difficult to convey the tone of quiet, well-argued

insistence of this Declaration in these snatches, but it does show how the people felt about Bruce.

To an extent it worked. The pope sent a stern letter to Edward II, and shortly afterwards officially recognised Bruce as king. There came a few peaceful years. Bruce thanked the Church, and the families who had helped him, with land grants, including Angus Og of the Isles. He made grants for the reconstruction of Melrose Abbey. So much did he spend that he had to ask a parliament at Cambuskenneth Abbey in July 1326 for an increase in his income. It was gladly given, and his little son David was formally recognised as his successor.

Elizabeth died on 26 October 1327. By the time he was fifty-six Bruce's own health was beginning to deteriorate. His illness has been labelled leprosy, but a more recent diagnosis of his symptoms suggests scurvy, a disease caused, as we now know, by an inadequate intake of vitamin C, which causes haemorrhages, infection and pain. Bruce became anxious to make his peace with God; guilt for the deaths of many people lay upon him, never expiated by a Crusade – regarded as a kind of soul-cleansing military pilgrimage.

Bruce spent his time pottering about his gardens and sailing on the Clyde. The pope at last lifted his Interdict on Scotland and his excommunication from Bruce, who set off on his last pilgrimage, as we have seen, to the shrine of St Ninian at Whithorn.

In May 1329 the peace concluded at Edinburgh was ratified by the English parliament and at last came acknowledgement of the independence of Scotland 'separate in all things from the kingdom of England'. This was welded by the marriage of two children, David aged four, and Edward III's seven-year-old sister Joan.

Then King Robert the Bruce lay down to die, summoning his friends to his bedside. He explained to them that his illness had been his penance for all the suffering he had caused others in his wars, and he told them about his vow to God that if he should manage to secure peace for his realm, he would go on a crusade.

Now that it was too late for him, would one of them please take his heart and go for him. James Douglas was chosen.

Tranter fictionalises an ancient tradition here. Bruce has made his farewells to most of his friends, and now it is the turn of Angus Og of the Isles. Bruce makes him 'dewar' of the Stone of Destiny. 'After my son's coronation, take it to your Isles, where none shall be able to follow it. And keep it safe, on some fair island. Until one of my line, or whoever is true King of Scots, requires it again for coronation.'

When Bruce finally breathed his last, on 7 June 1329, his body was embalmed. His heart was extracted and given to Sir James Douglas before the remains were carried in a splendid funeral procession across Scotland to Dunfermline Abbey for interment. 'And when the people knew that King Robert was dead, the sound of sorrow went from place to place.'

'Good' Sir James (The Black Douglas to the English) set Bruce's heart in an enamelled silver casket which he slung round his neck. He did go crusading, with six other knights. They went first to Spain and when his situation was clearly desperate, he is reputed to have hurled the heart into the midst of the attacking Moors before they killed him. Afterwards Bruce's heart was retrieved, and brought home along with Douglas's bones. Douglas was buried in the Kirk of Douglas, and Bruce's heart beneath the High Altar at Melrose Abbey. Professor Barrow describes Bruce as 'a potentate in the immemorial mould of the western Gaidhealtachd, inured since youth to a rough country and to rough warfare on land and sea . . . his grasp of tactics and strategy show him to have been much more than a guerilla leader, his governance was characterised by patience and a sense of justice . . . his picture of Scotland in the world was truly international, and his character had a peaceable, compassionate and humorous side which cannot but make those who read the sources warm to the man.'

Dunfermline Abbey goes back to the time of St Margaret, Malcolm Ceanmor's queen in the eleventh century. Bruce had helped the monks after their domestic buildings had been destroyed by the English in 1303. He was buried before the High Altar there, that summer of 1329, but by 1560, thanks to the Reformation, the buildings including its tombs had been wrecked. While work was being carried out to build a new church on the east end of the site, workmen found a vault containing human remains in an oak coffin. They were wrapped in a cloth-of-gold shroud and the breast bone had been severed, as for the extraction of the heart. At that time, a plaster cast of the skull was made. With great ceremony, and amid an upsurge of Scottish national feeling, Bruce was reinterred. Seventy years later one of his descendants, the Earl of Elgin, marked the place with a slab of Egyptian porphyry with medieval-style memorial brass embedded in it. Later, the head cast was used as the basis for sculptor Charles d'Orville Pilkington Jackson's famous Bannockburn statue.

At Melrose, an embalmed heart was removed from beneath the High Altar and transferred, for some strange reason, to the gardens beyond. In the summer of 1996 a lead casket was dug up there and taken for examination to an Edinburgh conservation laboratory. There ensued a lively debate about suggested reburial sites, ranging from Jerusalem, to a proposed Bruce Memorial Centre in Dumfries on which the local authority had already spent £100,000. Professor Duncan poured cold water on the rivals: 'There is a surviving letter, which I believe to be original, in which Bruce states that it was his intention that his heart ought to be buried at Melrose Abbey. There's no way that can be undone.'

Historic Scotland responded to the effect that it had strict guidelines on the treatment of human remains – that they should be reburied where they were found.

Today Robert the Bruce rides his bronze horse in triumph over the field of Bannockburn, his bones buried in Dumfermline Abbey, his heart beneath the green lawns of Melrose, and his lips forever sealed on the question of what he knows about the Stone of Destiny.

CHAPTER FIFTEEN

≈

THE STONE OF SKYE

After 1296 the Stone of Destiny leaves history and passes again into tradition and legend, cropping up in the folklore of several places in Scotland.

Early in the spring following Robert the Bruce's death, as we have seen in Chapter 15, a party of his friends led by Sir James Douglas left for the Crusades. One was absent: Angus Og of Islay. It is believed by some that Bruce, well aware that Scotland was in for another long regency, had asked him to take the Stone of Destiny into hiding.

Angus Og inherited Kintyre and Mull, but his brothers were either Comyn supporters or greedy for land. During Bruce's lifetime John MacDougall of Lorn, Comyn's son-in-law and proprietor of Dunstaffnage, had taken the opportunity of ambushing Bruce and his followers as they fled westward soon after the inauguration ceremony, through the narrow Pass of Brander in Argyll. Bruce only just escaped. Till then, he had been unsure of Angus Og's allegiance, but Angus arranged for a ship to spirit Bruce safely down the Clyde and handed over Dunaverty Castle to him, later persuading him to head for safety to Rathlin Island, off the north coast of Ireland. Angus's loyalty was tested. In revenge, John of Lorn ambushed him on his way to Mull. The following tale resulted, rediscovered and treasured by Danny Campbell of Bowmore, Islay. There isn't enough space for the whole of James Fyfe's ballad 'Donald O' Islay' (for Donald, read Angus), but a few stanzas give a flavour of it.

> O the castle yett is steekit fast
> An' sair tae speel is the castle wa';
> Ahint them deep i' the dungeon cast
> Lies Donald o' Islay, aince sae braw.

His raven locks are matted wi' gore,
His face is wan an' haggart an' worn;
Fu' length he lies on the cauld earth floor,
The wounded prisoner o' John o' Lorn.

The clansmen o' Lorn had ambush laid
I' the darkest neuk o' a lanesome glen,
Wi' hearts fu' o' veneance lang they stayed
Tae slay the noble Bruce an' his men.

An' first i' the Bruce's band sae sma'
Gaed Donald o' Islay brave an' true;
He led the gair, aye foremaist o' a',
Whaur red bluid flows an' whaur swords gleam blue.'

The fighting is detailed till the last moment:

An arrow had pierced his shouther deep,
An' he swooned awa' an' kent nae mair
Till he cam' tae i' the darksome keep,
Streek'd stiff an' sair on the earthen flair.'

Thrown into John of Lorn's deepest dungeon at Dunstaffnage, Angus languishes there till one day he is visited by the beautiful Sheila of Auchindell. She tells him she's being forced to wed Ian of Lorn, and that on her wedding day Angus is to be hanged – but takes him into her care anyway and nurses him back to health. She gazes up at him with her 'een sae blue' and whispers that she'd have preferred him for her bridegroom.

Then e'en as she spak', the soun' o' arms
On the castle wa's an' yett broke loose,
An' clear aboon a' the loud alarms
Rang the battle-cry 'A Bruce, A Bruce'.

Syne the chamber door was opened wide
An' Donald sank tae his bended knee,
For staun'in' there on the step ootside
Was the kingly Bruce, sae fair tae see.

An' a smile played owre his noble face:
Tae Donald he spak', an' thus spak' he:
'I've risked my life tae reach this place
I' the hope that I micht rescue thee,

'But I find ye noo' in bondage held
Faur stronger than Lorn could ever bind,
For nae chains that foe could ever weld
Can haud like the love o' woman kind.

'But quick through the glen we a' maun gang,
An' swift owre the muir we a' maun ride,
For I wou'dna' like tae see ye hang
Ere ye made this lady fair your bride.'

Bruce accompanies them thence to Islay where they are wed. Angus did become one of Bruce's most loyal friends, and, in thanks, Bruce passed Islay and the chieftainship of Clan Donald to him. From now on Angus was no longer his subject, but a near equal who supported Bruce of his own free will. After the success of Bannockburn, at which Angus Og fought well, Bruce rewarded him with more islands, along with Ardnamurchan, Glencoe, and part of Lochaber. Kintyre he kept for his own son.

According to Fordun, Angus Og *Ri Innse Gall* (King of the Isles of the Strangers) had two residences on Islay: his stronghold, Dunivaig Castle, which protected the south-east, and his hideaway fastness in Finlaggan Loch. Finlaggan was the place of inauguration and the centre of government for almost two centuries thereafter. The Stone of Destiny could have been kept in either. Dean Monro described how the Lords of the Isles often held counsel on the 'Ile of Finlaggan', and that it had been traditionally constructed, with 'ane fair chapell'. Only 'ane pennystane cast' away there was another, smaller, island 'callit in Irish Ellan na Comharle', on which was built the actual council house, in which fourteen 'Barons' 'decernit, decreitit and gave suits furth upon all debaitable matters according to the Laws.' He noted that in their day 'thair was great peace and welth in the Iles throw the ministration of justice.'

But the Stone Table around which they sat was 'carried away by Argyle with the bells that were at Icolumkill (Iona)'. This has been identified as the result of an expedition to Islay by the Marquess of Argyll about 1642. Other writers mention a Stone 2.1 metres square, bearing a footprint.

On Islay, in recent years, Dr David Caldwell and the Finlaggan Trust have been the focus of a ferment of archaeological interest as they excavate the stronghold of Angus's descendants, the Lords of the Isles. Two interesting if ambiguous stones have so far been identified on the site, but there is much digging yet to be done. Finlaggan Chapel is the best preserved of the buildings, being on higher ground because of its importance. The Counsel Isle, it turns out, is a crannog – a man-made island – on the end of an invisible underwater causeway discovered by Dr Caldwell in 1991. He also discovered a network of paved roads on Eilean Mòr, dated easily by the find of two groats of James III, minted in about 1485. On Eilean Mòr, beneath centuries-deep turf, Dr Caldwell's team discovered the ruins of the Great Hall (used for feasts and when other chiefs visited), its stores and service buildings, servants' quarters, two wells, guard houses by the jetty, the residence of the lord and his family, and an enclosure which was probably a garden. Cleanly carved graveslabs lie by the burial ground.

A team of archaeologists work with the Finlaggan Trust – Islay people such as retired teachers Rona and Donald McKenzie, Catriona Bell, ex-editor of the local newspaper *Ileach*, and her husband Donald who farms Finlaggan, and Mhairi McIntyre, crofter and another ex-editor of *Ileach*. Items are found – a fragment of chain-mail, and a harp-pin – which especially pleased Mhairi, for she feels it proves beyond doubt that Islay folk were never just 'a bunch of savages', but on the contrary, had always practised and enjoyed art and music.

'One of the 15th century graveslabs at Finlaggan has a flaw on the back of it which some believe is the foot-print stone,' writes Dr Caldwell. Above the western shore of the loch an outcrop of rock has a faint indentation, and others argue that this was the inaugural footprint because it is in the 'living' rock. 'I live in hope that that is still to be discovered,' he says of the Stone of Destiny.

His workers did dig up one large and delicately worked stone, which gave rise to tremendous excitement. Carved in the Iona workshops in Bruce's day or slightly later, it turned out to be the head of a cross. He says 'If I am right in my hunch, we will find the remnants of a very rich history, a continuity of occupation from pre-history up until the eighteenth century ... It is remarkable no serious attempt has been made to appreciate the story of Finlaggan.' He does not rule out the possibility that the Stone of Destiny may have been here, possibly used as the Counsel Table itself, and that it may turn up in future excavations. Meantime, in the summer months the little Visitor Centre is open and there is a tiny boat on a running-line in which one can pull oneself across to Eilean Mòr.

Angus Og operated like an Arthurian leader, his island lords around their Counsel Table. It was his son John who was first to be formally styled Lord of the Isles. It is clear that the Macdonalds had enjoyed absolute power, operating a kind of 'feudo-clanship', a mixture of landholding and kinship, and that John was inaugurated like a king, on a Stone. Only in detail was his ceremony different from that of the kings of Scots at Scone, such as that he wore a white habit, for innocence and integrity of heart and to suggest he would be a light to his people and maintain their religion. He received a white rod intimating that he had the power to rule with discretion and sincerity, and his forefathers' sword signifying that he would protect his people. Afterwards the white robe was given to his poet, by traditional right, and the feasting went on for a week. Fragments of the Book of the Dean of Lismore which dates from 1512, show Irish preoccupation with the old oral cycles like the stories of Tir-nan-og the land-of-the-ever-young beyond the sunset, and praise-songs sung by the seannachies till they were proscribed as 'sorners' (beggars) in 1612. Always there was the Celtic need for decoration, art, splendour and beauty. The Welsh historian Giraldus wrote in the twelfth century that the Scots harpers were 'the genuine source of the art'. They used quills, or their fingernails grown long for the purpose. They adorned their harps with silver and gems if possible, and those who were too poor used crystals instead. It becomes more and more inconceivable that a Stone revered by such a people would not be highly decorated and embellished.

Angus Og died at Finlaggan not long after Bruce in 1329. His body was taken to Iona for burial like his forebears. Three and a half centuries later, when the Lordship was forfeited, all their records were lost or destroyed. What happened to the Counsel Stone, and the Stone of Inauguration, on forfeiture? Peter Clarke wrote in the *Observer* about the dig, 'one of the best discoveries would be the Coronation Stone'.

Dr Caldwell is worried in case there is any truth in the tradition which says the Campbells removed a Stone from Finlaggan at the end of the seventeenth century, when they were quelling the MacDonalds, or that the Stone may have been broken up. If so, will the fragments be found when they dig deep into the Counsel Isle in the coming years? Could they have been built into the foundations of a nearby farmhouse? Or did the Macdonalds escape with their Stone after forfeiture and tranport it with them, in one of their famous galleys, to the isle of Skye? Did the Campbells have anything to do with it? At Inveraray Castle, Alastair Campbell of Airds, Unicorn Pursuivant, and the Chief Executive of Clan Campbell, admits that he has heard of the disappearance of the Counsel Stone from Finlaggan, says there is no trace of either the Stone or of tales about it at Inveraray, and reminds us that it was the Campbells of Cawdor who became the owners of Islay in the seventeenth century.

If the Stone is not found on Islay, where might the Macdonalds have taken it? After Angus Og's descendants forfeited their Lordship they led seven major risings to restore it, but the death of Domhnall Dubh in 1545 put an end to their hopes. There remains a tradition that, when one branch of Clan Donald took over the Sleat Peninsula of Skye in the seventeenth century, the Stone went with them. The secret of exactly where they've kept it is supposedly handed down from father to son. Stories about it variously suggest that it is kept in a cave, or hidden by a waterfall. The only problem about this legend is that the chief of the clan, Lord Macdonald, gives the impression he knows nothing about it. But of course he wouldn't, would he, if it's a family secret?

Armadale Castle is now the magnificent Clan Centre of the Macdonalds. No written records about the Stone have been found there. But branches of the clan are scattered over the globe, so it was only mildly surprising when, in the 1950s, a series of letters turned up, written by a young man who claimed secret knowledge of the Skye Stone's whereabouts.

This particular letter-writer, born in India but living at that time in Brighton, had just sufficient intriguing fact to catch the imagination, amongst a hotch-potch of information and misinformation. He signed himself 'C. Iain Alasdair Macdonald'.

The excerpts from his letters are quoted as they were written, so that spelling, style and tone can be taken into consideration along with content.

The first arrived in April 1959, on crested notepaper showing a rampant bird, a ship, and the motto *per mare per terras*: 'I have in my possession an antique chest which has been handed down . . . through generations of Macdonalds of the Isles and which dates back to Somerled, Regulus of the Isles . . . In the secret place [on Skye] where the chest was originally hidden is also "The Stone" which I believe is the "Stone of Destiny" . . . I may add that I myself am decended from Macdonalds of the Isles. My family hailing from Sleate.'

The next letter said: 'I am now the custodian of "The Stone" and have seen it myself and know its hiding place in Skye. I was brought from India by my Grandfather and father to Skye and taken to the secret hiding place and shown the

Stone, which I sat on and made to take the oath to guard its secret whereabouts and also to screen my sucessor.

'So well is it hidden that I was taken four times along the secret route and then find my own way four times to make sure I had a clear picture in my mind – of the route stone by stone. I went again myself after discharge from the forces after the war in 1946 which took me quite a while to find my way . . .

"The Stone" which measures approx 11 in by 21 in is supposed to be resting in its origional seating of marble but presume half of it is missing. The Stone as far as I can make out resembles a well filled pillow and has many weird superstitions – rather amusing. My Grandfather often said its like no known stone he has ever seen and he was widly travelled. He said "Heaven alone knows where it origionated" Having seen it and sat on it, I have no doubts about it being the real thing. My mind takes me back to my first aquaintance with it and never shall I forget the experience as I sat on it – before I knew what it really was.'

In another letter Macdonald offers his pedigree as evidence of his right to the secret of the whereabouts of the Stone of Destiny, citing a long genealogy and quoting a secret document found in the chest. He says of his ancestors, with varying factual accuracy; 'Somerled made many attempts to capture the Merble chair or Stone of destiny of Kennth Macalpin. It was not until 1329 as Bruce lay dying, that John, eldest son of Angus, and his followers brought the stone of Destiny to Skye.

'John was crowned Regulus of the Isles in the year 1354. John when he assumed power turned out to be a drunken lout. His drunken orgies . . . brought great displeasure and disgrace on the clan. He was cruel to his little wife Amy, who feared for her life. Most of John's followers having deserted him, helped Amy to escape with their young son Donald whom John was seeking to murder one terrible March night during one of his drunken orgies. They fled to the Monastery of Sadell. Amy's followers brought the Stone, the Oaken Kist of Somerled, the Golden Circlet, Bracelets and Collar of Somerled.

'John divorced his wife Amy. Donald 2 was brought up in the ways of the Lord. He was anointed and crowned Regulus of the Isles at 12 years old in the years of Grace 1366 by Father John of Sadell. During the Banquet, the golden Collar of an hundred peices of fine gold, was stolen from the sleeping prince while resting in his bedchambder believed by Robert high Steward of Scotland and John . . . never recovered . . . Hear endeth the certified true copy of the origional manuscript written by the monks of Sadell now tattered and in peices and almost unreadable . . .

'. . . 'The Stone' known as "Lia Fail" or Stone of Destiny is this day with the Oaken Kist containing the golden Circlet, Golden Bracelet set with precious stones, removed to a place of great secrecy. known only to the eldest son in direct blood sucession. Hear the secret will be kept even under penalty of death.

'Set by my hand this twenty third day of March in the year of Grace seventeen hundred and twenty. Calean Macdonald. fifteenth prince of the Isles and of Sleat.'

Macdonald included a sketch drawn from memory of his Stone.

At Register House in Edinburgh experts were intrigued, but thought the lettering and the phraseology suggested that the manuscript was unlikely to be genuine – at least at its date of 1720. Margaret Macdonald, Curator of the Library at the Clan Donald Centre, agrees that the family tree is faulty. Clearly the letter-writer is not connected with the present Macdonalds of Sleat, yet he does seem genuinely to have believed he had some claim to a family relic. What motivated him to give this secret away? Why divulge a valuable piece of family information to an individual one doesn't even know? Could he have been trying to get back at a relative who had denied him an inheritance, or recognition? Was he perhaps the black sheep of the family? Had he come back from the war warped in some way – a crank? Or is there a flavour of truth in what he wrote? Strenuous efforts have been made to trace him over the years, through the good offices of Somerset House, and a variety of newspapers and journals, but all have failed. Did he exist? Was he writing under a pseudonym – and if so, why?

There may be other sources of information about Skye and its Stone awaiting study. At the time of the Reformation many church documents were sent from Scotland to the Vatican for safe-keeping. They are still there, now being more closely scrutinised by scholars, and they do give valuable information. Dr Norman Macdougall of St Andrews University mentions in his magnificent biography (1989) that James IV travelled to the islands. The reasons are not specified, but there is a legend that he went in order to have himself properly crowned on the Stone there.

Professor Cowan talks of Scottish information buried in other places; of how inconvenient it is to have material in, for instance, Corpus Christi College, Cambridge, the Vatican and Paris. 'Most of these documents are not originals, but copies. We don't know how the originals were dispersed or looted, but these collections seem to have originated with antiquaries in the seventeenth and eighteenth centuries.' Asked if they're being actively studied at the moment he replies, 'No. They're just kept. But we have a big project run out of this department, which is to collect all the Scottish material out of the Vatican archive – it's all here on microfilm now. It's really hard to read. The Poppleton Manuscript in the Bibliothèque Nationale in Paris is a chronicle which has a number of early Scottish annals embedded in it, but it's not a Scottish document, it was put together in York by somebody in the north of England, probably with reference to the propaganda wars that went on during the wars of Independence. But we can get copies of it.' He feels there is much work to be done on these and other old documents.

If there is indeed a Stone on Skye, where might it be hidden? Margaret Macdonald, of the Clan Donald library, suggested a search round Loch nam Uamh, the Loch of the Cave, which lies in the hills to the north of Armadale. After a lot of walking and searching however, no cave was to be found there, but the terrain is rock and bog, and caves can be blocked with mud, or entrances closed off deliberately with boulders. Yet another tradition turned up though, that once, many years ago, there was a secret tunnel from somewhere near Tarskavaig through which you could reach Loch nam Uamh. Possibly this was an old mineworking. There are caves on Sleat, in particular on the north-west coast, and in the cliffs to the south-east, and a stone could very easily be hidden in one of these.

And of course there is the other possibility. Whenever a mere lowlander goes looking for something in the Highlands, be it an illicit still or a lost stone, as we saw in Chapter 2 when the unfortunate Sassenachs were given the run-around by Kay Matheson and her friends, he is liable to be given less than helpful response to his questions. He is likely to be answered by locals with their Gaelic tongues firmly planted in their cheeks, who are not about to divulge the well-kept secrets of the Gaeltachd to any mere 'foreigner'. The more drams the researcher tries to bribe them with, the better the laugh the Gaels can have behind their hands as they recount the tale.

There may, then, be a mysterious Stone hiding in a cave on Skye. It may be the case that somebody knows its whereabouts – or it may have been taken into the care of a secret organisation. For the Skye Macdonalds have a strong connection with the Knights Templar, a body of men who say they are the true keepers of the Stone.

≈

CHAPTER SIXTEEN

THE KNIGHTS TEMPLAR

For many centuries, descendants of Angus Og and other well-connected Scottish families have been members of an organisation known nowadays as the Ordugh Rioghail Cathachail Teampuill Ierusalem – the Scottish Knights Templar – who are interested in several ancient Stones. They even bought a church for the safe-keeping of one stone in particular.

Nine Crusaders founded the Order of Poor Knights of Christ and the Temple of Solomon in Jerusalem in 1118, their purpose to police the pilgrim routes to the Holy Land. King Baldwin II of Jerusalem was so pleased that he gave them space in his palace – reputedly built over the ruins of Solomon's Temple – hence their name. Young European nobles rushed to join. Its ideals were Arthurian: oaths of chastity, obedience and poverty were sworn which turned the boys out as military monks, highly skilled fighters in touch with God, obliged to fight to the death. They didn't shave, and wore uniform white surcoats emblazoned with a splayed scarlet cross front and back. Responsible only to the pope, they became known as the Knights Templar, and people showered them with gifts and privileges.

Invited by King David I to be 'the custodian of his morals' – and a useful bodyguard – they arrived in Scotland in 1128. Eventually Templars held over five hundred Scottish properties, and in England one of their typical circular churches can still be seen at The Temple, London. The Stone features in the records of both the Knights Templar and Scottish Freemasonry.

When the Holy Land fell to the Saracens in 1291, the Knights had to find a new raison d'être. By 1306 their wildness and power was scaring Philip IV of France, who persuaded Pope Clement V to excommunicate them, and the Order was finished in Europe. There are those who believe this is why the Knights were in a position to alter the balance of power between Scotland and England in the early fourteenth century. Bishop William Lamberton of St Andrews had been ordered by both Edward II of England and the pope to weed the Templars out of Scotland. But Lamberton remained utterly loyal to the excommunicated Robert the Bruce and to Scottish independence. There is a suggestion that, far from interrogating two Templars at Holyrood in December 1309, Lamberton came to an arrangement with them: sanctuary in Scotland in return for arms, money and expertise. Papal Bulls were not being proclaimed in Scotland, therefore the Templars could not legally be dissolved there. They had stockpiles of armaments in Ireland, and shipping to bring them over. Edward II is on record complaining about the import of arms to Scotland at this time.

A group of thirteenth-century masons, later known as the 'Loch Awe School', carved graveslabs showing warriors carrying swords – the unmistakable sign of a Templar's grave. These are unique to Argyll and its islands. The ships depicted are different from west-coast galleys of the period. Are they mementoes of the lost Templar fleet?

Sir Iain Bosville Macdonald of Sleat and many others have agreed it is highly likely that Bruce was assisted at Bannockburn by the Templars. Studies of contemporary methods of warfare, descriptions of the battle and of Bruce's style of fighting demonstrate Templar strategies and techniques, not seen in Scotland before.

Bruce commanded only about 6000 men, mainly infantry. At a time when foot-soldiers were usually poorly organised, Bruce's army was disciplined and astonishingly well equipped, each man having a leather headpiece and steel helmet, thickly padded leather coat, flexible steel gloves for holding his iron-tipped twelve foot spear, a knife, an axe and a sword.

Such weaponry cost far more than Bruce could have scraped from his coffers, with Scotland's economy in ruins, and many of his wealthy lowland nobles believing it would serve their interests better to fight for England. Bruce, desperate for reconciliation with the Pope, daren't record Templar help, and Archdeacon Barbour would have edited out of his epic poem *The Brus* an order whose name was anathema to his church.

What happened to the Templars in Scotland after that? There is some evidence that the ensuing secret society made a useful information grapevine for Jacobite nobles. Certain Scottish lords are to this day involved in freemasonry. A Templar cross was reputedly found on Graham of Claverhouse when he died at Killiecrankie in 1689.

A mason's set-square and a Templar's Cross are portrayed on a gravestone at Kilmory, Argyll, demonstrating the link between Templar and Mason. There are strong connections with Melrose Abbey, too, whose insignia includes the Rose and the Mell, or mason's hammer. The Knights Templar still meet at Melrose once a year.

The late Chaplain of Dundee Preceptory was Chevalier the Reverend John Mackay Nimmo, a keen Scottish Nationalist. In the early 1990s the Templars bought a little church in the pretty village of Dull, near Aberfeldy. In it they installed a stone that they had had in their possession for almost thirty years, and which they say is the Stone of Destiny recovered from Westminster Abbey in 1950. It was found in Parliament Square in Edinburgh in 1965 and kept by Revd Nimmo in his church – St Columba's – at Lochee in Dundee, where it lay in an iron cage for all to see. The Revd Nimmo affirmed that this was the real Stone. 'Baillie Gray, a friend of mine, annealed the Stone – put the two parts together . . . We had a mobbed service at the reception of the Stone [in Dundee]. My wife said, "Come on Baillie, tell us the truth" and he said, "Lassie, do you think I would take part in this kind of a service over a phoney stone? No, no. This is the real Stone of Destiny."'

When St Columba's Church was closed in 1990 the Stone was sent for safe keeping into the charge of Elspeth King, then Curator of the People's Palace Museum in Glasgow. Did it contain bronze dowels – a prerequisite to prove it was the one mended by Baillie Gray? Materials testing consultants Harry Stanger Ltd offered to find out. Their tests gave print-outs that told all that needed to be known about what lay hidden inside that Stone. Ian Hamilton came over to the People's Palace from the High Court to keep an eye on the proceedings.

Meanwhile a seer, Sweyn Macdonald of Ardgay in Easter Ross, who has had the second sight since he was a boy, and who is himself a trained stonemason, recalled a night in the 1960s. Like a Knox delivering the Truth he declared 'You couldn't make a King without a Stone – that was their belief. The one I saw would be about three-quarters of a hundredweight – a block of grey sandstone about eighteen inches by twelve, four or five inches high. The edges are smooth, no marks, worn like a doorstep, a slight wear in the centre as if it could have been used for stepping on, a little hollow – maybe it was water dripping on it. I was involved with a crowd of Scottish Nationalists in Edinburgh. We do need a parliament in Edinburgh. We were having a discussion and the Stone came up. Two or three days later I was invited to an old ruined place and I was shown the real Stone. They brought it out and let me see it to prove it to me. There's another one that was made to represent it. There's only three people at a time that is allowed to know the exact whereabouts of that Stone – if two were killed there's a third to hand it on. You are the first person that I've ever told – not even my close family. It belongs to a Scottish organisation.'

'The Knights Templar?'

'You said that, lass, I didn't. There's another Stone, older than that – I saw two of them. Near Scone Palace. In that area. They brought it out for me – I didn't see the exact place where it was hidden. And I tell you, lass, it will never be discovered until – until we have our Home Rule. The Stone has to remain hidden because I know that if the English got it they'd take it away and destroy it.'

At present there are some 150 members of the Scottish Knights Templar, including ministers, headmasters and academics. They possess a secret, alternative version of Scotland's history, contained in their 'Stella Templum', which refers to four Stones: St Columba's Seat, the Pictish Stone, the Celtic Stone, and the Stone of Destiny. They do not tell the public at large where these are kept. Filmed inside Rosslyn Chapel for BBC's Ex-S programme in 1996, one of their membership, John Ritchie, announced that the Stone of Destiny never left Scotland. He talked of 'equations' which cannot be described in words that tell the Knights how to find it when the right time comes.

If the Knights Templar exhibit one Stone, where are the other three – do they, in fact, exist? For no one so far has been able to describe them. It would be good if someone could persuade the Knights to release photographs or drawings of these mysterious objects, in the interests of accuracy and truth. Having such a relatively unbroken link with the legendary past of Scotland, they would seem to be particularly well-placed to inform and educate the rest of us, especially on the subject of Stones of Destiny. But perhaps what is needed, instead, is a more scientific approach.

≈

CHAPTER SEVENTEEN

SIR WALTER SCOTT AND EDINBURGH CASTLE

As far as the general public was concerned, the Stone languished on through the centuries in Westminster Abbey. Monarch after monarch was crowned upon it. Any person who might have known of the whereabouts of any alternative Stone was either dead or sworn to very effective secrecy. And yet it was not entirely forgotten.

Instead, the Stone began to rematerialise, first as just a sentence here and there in a history book, then growing to occupy the space of a few paragraphs in the work of a master story-teller.

Walter Scott was born in College Wynd, Edinburgh, in 1771, at a time when Scottish literature was coming into its own. Educated at Edinburgh High School, he studied law at Edinburgh University, and by the time he was called to the Bar, aged twenty-one, several writers were busy putting Scotland on the literary map. At thirty-three, Robert Burns was the toast of the capital after the success of his first, 'Kilmarnock Edition', collection of poems. Fifty-one year-old Edinburger James Boswell had published his famous Journal.

Before Scott was forty, Jane Porter was writing her 'modern romance', *Scottish Chiefs* (1810). This book about 'the sister kingdoms' of England and Scotland became highly popular – clearly its subject matter struck a chord with readers. It was translated into Russian and German, and brought her fan letters from Moscow to India. Napoleon even denounced it as 'dangerous to the state' and blocked its French publication. Beginning with the murder of Lady

Wallace, it follows the fortunes of the Stone, and ends with Bannockburn.

In her preface Porter expresses the feeling of the day:

It is now too common to contemn [sic] as nonsense even an honest pride in ancestry . . . Happy it is for this realm that the destiny which now unites the once contending arms of those brave families has also consolidated their rival nations into one, and by planting the heir of Plantagenet and of Bruce upon one throne, hath redeemed the peace of Britains, and fixed it on lasting foundations.

Happy thought indeed.

A great flowering of science and philosophy was taking place at this time. The bitter pill of Union had been swallowed, General Wade's roads had made the countryside of Scotland accessible – and controllable – the Jacobites had been sent packing and peace reigned. Meanwhile Madame Guillotine was chopping up French aristocrats, in America President George Washington was building his White House; in India Ranjit Singh ruled; Russia was grabbing Black Sea resorts from the Turks and helping itself to Poland, and Austria was being aggressive all over Europe.

Scott was fascinated by Scottish history, and wrote reams about it. In 1805 he published *The Lay Of The Last Minstrel*, and ten years later *Lord Of The Isles*. During this period he bought and rebuilt his beloved house on the Tweed, near Melrose. He called it Abbotsford. He first enthusiastically recounted his history of Scotland to Johnnie Lockhart, alias 'Hugh Littlejohn Esq', his six-year-old grandson, as they rode together under the summer trees by the river. These *Tales of a Grandfather* (1827) are full of warmth and affection.

Scott begins by explaining 'How Scotland and England came to be separate Kingdoms' before their union. By Chapter 6 he has reached the fateful year of 1296.

Edward marched through Scotland at the head of a powerful army, compelling all ranks of people to submit to him. He removed to London the records of the kingdom of Scotland, and was at pains to transport to the Abbey Church at Westminster a great stone, upon which it had been the national custom to place the King of Scotland when he was crowned for the first time. He did this to show that he was absolute master of Scotland ... The stone is still preserved, and to this day the King's throne is placed upon it at the time when he is crowned. Last of all, King Edward ... placed English soldiers in all the castles and strongholds of Scotland, from the one end of the kingdom to the other, and not trusting the Scots themselves, he appointed English governors in most of the provinces of the kingdom ... Perhaps Edward thought to himself that, by uniting the whole island of Britain under one king and one government, he would do so much good by preventing future wars, as might be an excuse for the force and fraud which he made use of to bring about his purpose. But, my dear child ... We must not do evil even that good may come of it; and the happy prospect that England and Scotland would be united under one government, was so far from being brought nearer by Edward's unprincipalled usurpation, that the hatred and violence of national antipathy which arose betwixt the sister countries, removed to a distance almost incalculable, the prospect of their becoming one people, for which nature seemed to design them.

Scott adds a footnote:

This fatal stone was said to have been brought from Ireland by Fergus, the son of Eric, who led the Dalriads to the shores of Argyleshire. Its virtues are preserved in the celebrated leonine verse '*Ni fallat fatum* ...' etc which may be rendered thus:-

> Unless the fates are faithless found,
> And prophets' voice be vain,
> Where'er this monument is found
> The Scottish race shall reign.

There were Scots who hailed the accomplishment of this prophecy at the accession of James VI to the crown of England, and exulted, that in removing this palladium, the policy of Edward resembled that which brought the Trojan horse in triumph within their walls, and which occasioned the destruction of their royal family.

In fact, while Edward 1 stayed in the Castle on 14th June 1296 – before he went to Scone – he forced his way into the royal treasuries of Scotland. There, as we saw in Chapter 13, he selected such things as he thought proper to be removed as spoils of war, partly to enrich his own treasury and partly, as with Wales, to remove the central nervous system of the lively body that Scotland had once been – to break the Scottish spirit. He removed or destroyed all the kingdom's ancient records. These are shown in an inventory, *Inventa in Castro de Edenburgh* along with those he had taken a few years before at Norham. He also took the Crown and Sceptre and the other insignia of sovereignty.

On his way south from Scone, Edward arrived back in Edinburgh on Friday 17 August 1296. One account details that he 'sent three chests of the royal records to London, so much as could be found of the royal plate, the Black Rood of his ancestress St Margaret, and the crowning stone that Fergus, first king of Dalriada, had brought from Ireland.'

On 26th March 1707, when the Scottish parliament was adjourned, the Honours of Scotland – the Scottish crown jewels – were taken to Edinburgh Castle, to be locked away in an oak chest which was supposedly sealed into a vault and walled up – and forgotten about. Many believed the Honours had in fact been secretly removed to England. Over a hundred years later, on 4th February 1818, armed with a Royal Warrant, accompanied by the Officers of State, Scott supervised the breaking down of the walls. The group watched in silence.

As an antiquarian, Scott had been campaigning for this moment. Inside the vault lay a huge wooden chest. He wrote:

> The chest seemed to return a hollow and empty sound to the strokes of the hammer, and even those whose expectations had been most sanguine felt at the moment the probability of disappointment . . . The joy was therefore extreme when, the ponderous lid of the chest being forced open, the Regalia

were discovered lying at the bottom covered with linen cloths
... The discovery was instantly communicated to the public
by the display of the Royal Standard, and was greeted by
shouts of the soldiers in the garrison, and a vast multitude
assembled on the Castle Hill; indeed the rejoicing was so
general and sincere as plainly to show that, however altered
in other respects, the people of Scotland had lost nothing of
that national enthusiasm which formerly had displayed itself
in grief for the loss of these emblematic Honours, and now
was expressed in joy for their recovery.

The Edinburgh *Evening Courant* announced, '150 Persons
only will be admitted every lawful day' at a cost per person
of one shilling.

The years 1818 and 1819 saw a tremendous surge of interest
in Scottish history. Scott and other antiquaries may have been
called in to examine a mysterious stone found at Edinburgh
Castle and some suggest that this might have been the original
Stone of Destiny. Some say Scott positively identified it.

Yet his writings show that, being a balanced sort of a person
and no nationalist, Scott was not above having a healthy laugh
at the expense of his compatriots from time to time. He was a
known practical joker, and found opportunities for mischief
quite irresistible. On one occasion he even published a paper on
a 'prehistoric rock carving' near Yarrow for the Proceedings of
the Society of Antiquaries of Scotland, only recently debunked
in that august publication by rock expert Ronald Morris.

Could the Stone still lie hidden in Edinburgh Castle? It is
possible that the real one did arrive there from Scone, but that
in the ten days or so that elapsed between its removal from
Scone and Edward's return to Edinburgh or between then and
its despatch southward, some enterprising soul swapped it for
the fake that went to Westminster – in which case the original
may be there yet, hidden in some other unopened dungeon.

On Scott's own way into history, his writings influenced
many people, not least Queen Victoria who created her
Highland home at Balmoral and made Scotland fashionable.
He also encouraged his fellow-writers, with generosity and

foresight; in 1813 Scott refused a proffered Laureateship for himself and recommended the poet Southey instead. He discovered James Hogg, the 'Ettrick Shepherd' (1770–1835), who had helped him with material for his Border Minstrelsy. Scott's success encouraged a variety of Scottish enterprises. The Gaelic-speaking son of a Kingussie farmer, James MacPherson (1736–96), 'translated' Ossian's poetry to acclaim from Goethe and challenge from Dr Johnson, but was popular enough to be buried in Westminster Abbey. William Blackwood thought it worth his while to start a magazine in 1817, and in 1882 the Scottish Text Society was founded, which then began to publish rare manuscripts such as Barbour's *The Brus*.

Sir Walter Scott may not have found the Stone of Destiny itself, but he was responsible for keeping alive an interest in Scottish history, myth and legend, and as a result much has survived in popular culture that would otherwise have withered and died for lack of love.

And it was during Scott's lifetime that an interesting Stone was dug up in Perthshire.

CHAPTER EIGHTEEN

MACBETH'S CASTLE

O n New Year's Day 1819, while Sir Walter Scott was
busily stirring up interest in Scottish history, when
amateur archaeology was beginning to become popular,
and when writers and poets were taking a new interest in
myth and legend, *The Times* published: '*Macbeth's Castle –
(Curious Discovery)*'. A letter from Dunsinane, in Scotland,
states as follows:-

On the 19th November, as the servants belonging to the West
Mains of Dunsinane house, were employed in carrying away
stones from the excavation made among the ruins that point
out the site of Macbeth's Castle here, part of the ground they
stood on suddenly gave way, and sunk down about six feet,
discovering a regularly built vault, about six feet long and four
wide. None of the men being injured, curiosity induced them
to clear out the subterranean recess, when they discovered
among the ruins a large stone, weighing about 500l, which
is pronounced to be of the meteoric or semi-metallic kind.
This stone must have lain here during the long series of ages
since Macbeth's reign.

Besides it were also found two round tablets, of a
composition resembling bronze. On one of these two lines
are engraved, which a gentleman has thus deciphered – 'The
sconce (or shadow) of kingdom come, until sylphs in air carry
me again to Bethel.' These plates exhibit the figures of targets
for the arms. 'From time immemorial it has been believed
among us here, that unseen hands brought Jacob's pillow
from Bethel, and dropped it on the site where the palace of
Scoon now stands. A strong belief is also entertained by many
in this part of the country, that it was only a representation
of this Jacob's pillow that Edward sent to Westminster, the
sacred stone not having been found by him. The curious here,
aware of such traditions, and who have viewed these venerable
remains of antiquity, agree that Macbeth may, or rather must,

have deposited the stone in question at the bottom of his Castle, on the hill of Dunsinane (from the trouble of the times), where it has been found by the workmen . . .

On the following day the same letter appeared in the *Morning Chronicle*, and throughout January it was to appear in several other newspapers, including the *Edinburgh Evening Chronicle*, the *Glasgow Herald*, and the *Caledonian Mercury*. The letter is, in every case, unattributed. Is its credibility therefore in doubt? Could it have been a Ne'erday hoax? One has to admit that possibility. And yet – does the ring of truth not echo down the ages, 'from time immemorial it has been believed among us here . . .'?

There is an earlier source of the tradition. Seton Gordon quotes a story passed down through the Earls of Mansfield, hereditary owners of Scone Palace:

> Somewhere around the dates 1795–1820, a farm lad had been wandering with a friend on Dunsinnan . . . soon after a violent storm. The torrential rain had caused a small landslide, and as the result of this a fissure, which seemed to penetrate deep into the hillside was visible. The two men procured some form of light and explored the fissure. They came at last to the broken wall of a subterranean chamber. In one corner of the chamber was a stair which was blocked with debris, and in the centre of the chamber they saw a slab of stone covered with hieroglyphics and supported by four short stone legs. As there was no evidence of 'treasure' in the subterranean apartment the two men did not realise the importance of their find and did not talk of what they had seen.
>
> Some years later one of the men first heard the local tradition that on the approach of King Edward I the monks of Scone hurriedly removed the Stone of Destiny to a place of safe concealment and took from the Annety Burn a stone of similar size and shape, which the English king carried off in triumph. When he heard this legend the man hurried back to Dunsinnan Hill, but whether his memory was at fault regarding the site of the landslide, or whether the passage of time, or a fresh slide of earth, had obliterated the cavity, the fact remains that he was unable to locate the opening in the hillside.

Seton Gordon discusses the question of why the thirteenth century monks of Scone had not returned the Stone to the abbey after Edward had gone: 'the tradition accounts for this by explaining that it was not considered safe at the time to allow the English to know that they had been tricked, and that when the days of possible retribution were past the monks who had known the secret were dead.'

In 1819, in spite of the famous Enlightenment, ordinary Scots were a cowed people, many were still being cleared from the land in favour of sheep and exported by the boat-load to the colonies, others were seeking their fortunes in India – newly colonised into the British Empire – to become yet another area to be printed in pink-for-British on the world map. London was perceived as the epicentre of government, of manners and of speech.

But the old story-telling tradition was still very much a part of everyday life at all levels of society, and not only in Scotland. The Perthshire legend of Dunsinnan, like others of its kind, is likely to have grown from a grain of truth.

Why was the letter not attributed in any of the papers? Because it was considered vulgar for writers to publicise their names. Even famous novelists like Scott and Dickens would serialise their work anonymously.

Was the *Times* letter written by a group of jokers? This seems unlikely, because the personality of an individual shines through, the tone neither pompous nor facetious, the writer clearly feeling that the servants not being injured was worthy of report. He knew something of Scottish history, but the inaccuracy about Macbeth shows this knowledge was faulty, so perhaps the writer was not an academic, though the language is that of a reasonably well-educated person. He reports what the servants experienced – not that he himself witnessed the event described. His attitude is dated, too, showing no idea of archaeological stratification, whereby sites are layered according to successive waves of occupation; he supposed that all the finds were laid down at one time. The

fact that so many newspaper editors gave the letter space that
January shows that they believed the entire reading population
of Britain would be interested in its contents.

For some unstated reason, that year Dr James Playfair, Principal of St Andrews University, suddenly undertook an excavation
of Macbeth's Castle on Dunsinnan Hill, which, as he wrote: 'lies
in the Sidla ridge, 7 miles SSW of Cupar . . . of a conical form,
1024 feet above the level of the sea'. His report is almost exactly
the wording of the anonymous entry in the *Statistical Account*
which is generally accepted to be also written by him:

> Its summit is an oval area 210 feet from east to west, and
> 130 feet in breadth; which M. fortified with a strong rampart
> of stone, cemented with red mortar. Penetrating horizontally
> seven yards into the ruins of this rampart, I lately discovered
> a part of it as entire as when it was originally constructed.
> Founded with rock, it is neatly built of large stones. If the
> rubbish on the outside were removed this would be one of
> the most remarkable monuments of antiquity in Britain. At
> the foot of that wall there was a level walk of considerable
> breadth, and 231 yards in circuit secured by a parapet and
> ditch. Having diligently explored the area of the fortress, now
> 3 feet below the surface, and cut a deep trench across it, I found
> no vestige of buildings in it; so the temporary houses were
> probably composed of wood. In one corner great quantities
> of charcoal, bones of black cattle, sheep and hares were dug
> up, but none of the human body. From the summit of this
> hill, there is a delightful prospect of Strathmore, the Lomond
> hills, Birnam Hill and part of Strathearn. The fortress was
> demolished in the year 1057.

This was the first of several archaeological digs on Dunsinnan
Hill. Each one was to find a little more evidence than the others,
and each left a trail of wreckage in its wake. The *Times* letter-
writer's inexactitude about Macbeth's dates – he reigned in the
eleventh century – gave two people food for creative thought.

Ten years after its publication, Robert Chambers is enjoying
the thought that Shakespeare himself had visited this place
'and thus became personally acquainted with the localities
of the tragedy which he afterwards wrote upon the story

of Macbeth' and that therefore 'the traveller will consider Dunsinnan as holy ground'. Chambers makes a point about the ruined rampart, 'the height of which is conjectured to have been considerable, from the immense mass remaining' – a factor agreed upon by archaeologists today – and goes on to discuss 'Mr Nairne of Dunsinnan' and his findings: 'A theory has been started, in consequence of Mr Nairne's discovery, that Macbeth, from an implicit faith in the sacred character of the stone, and that the possession of it would insure the continuance of his sovereignty, transferred it to a close concealment in his fortress, subsituting in its place a similar stone, which has ever since been accepted as the real one.' According to Chambers then, no less than twelve Scottish kings would have been crowned on Macbeth's replacement stone at Scone before Edward I got it.

The second writer describes Nairne's dig and agrees:

> It has been supposed that Macbeth may, or rather must have deposited the real Simon Pure [meaning the original Stone of Destiny] in the foundations of his castle, as he would deem its possession of great importance, as a supernatural aid to keep him on his usurped throne, and that to prevent it being purloined he buried it in the foundations of his castle, where it was found in 1818. All this is pleasing and fanciful; but assuming it to be true, we must conclude that Macbeth on removing it from its original site, had substituted another one resembling it in its stead, and this one would be the stone carried off by Edward I to Westminster Abbey. It is a pity that Mr Nairne did not get the inscription engraved and published, as it is very likely the translation given is incorrect.

By 1850 James Myles is waxing lyrical about Macbeth's exploits on Dunsinnan Hill, and showing continued interest in the Stone, relating the Nairne story almost verbatim from previous accounts. Five years later a paper is read, at the April meeting of the Society of Antiquaries of Scotland, in which Nairne's excavations and several findings are reported, and a diagram shown of the structure of the ruins on top of the hill. In 1857 the Society reports:

Upon digging, last year, into the south-east side of the top of the hill, and several feet under the grass covering, four rude chambers were found built of freestone, generally of old red sandstone, some of the varieties of which seem to have been brought from a considerable distance. The stones were all undressed, and carefully built ... On examining these chambers more carefully, they were found to occupy a quadrangular space and to communicate with each other by small passages, two feet broad, by three in height ...The southern wall ... was nearly straight, and was probably the outer wall stated by Principal Playfair to be 5 or 6 feet in height ... This wall extended backward ... forming two chambers 20 feet in length, having two entrances ... These chambers had usually a rounded figure, were 7 or 8 feet in diameter; and after the wall had been raised 2 or 3 feet above the stone flooring of the chamber, the stones overlapped each other as the building advanced upwards, so as to form a roof, which was completed by a large flat stone placed over the top, the rude substitute for an arch. The greatest height of these chambers was 6 feet from the floor, which was laid with undressed flags. As the roofs of these chambers had fallen in, or their walls had been disturbed by former excavations, it was not always easy to discover their original figures, particularly as they were filled with black earth and stones, the accumulation of ages ... the passage ... between the inner chambers ... was built up, and on opening it three skulls were found with a number of fragments of human bones.

The bodies had been placed in a sitting position, with the knees pushed up to the chin. They were 'a 60 year-old woman, an adult male, an adult female and a young child, a female, apparently murdered'.

In 1871 the Revd Thomas Brown, Minister of Collace, is reporting T. M. Nairne's find of a small spiral bronze ring in the form of a serpent: 'the eyes and scales on the back being carved in the most minute manner ... it was only when they were looked at through a microscope that their beauty and exquisite workmanship became apparent'. It was found while a trench was being dug near the gateway of the fort, 'lying on the surface of the earth and rubbish which had been thrown up while the digging was going on'. This shows that at least one of the people who fled up to Macbeth's castle for safety, or who used it for aggression, appreciated art, craft and beautiful things. Sadly it also demonstrates the state of archaeological understanding at the time, as workmen spaded out 'rubbish'. The carelessness of the day is also in evidence; the ring was given to Mr Nairne, who managed to lose it after only a year.

But a doorway was discovered on Dunsinnan,

> consisting of two rude unhewn slabs forming the posts, and a similar slab forming the lintel. From the doorway, which was low and narrow, and could not have been entered by a man in an upright position, there was a sloping passage leading to what seemed to be a house or burrow of considerable size, but underground; so that, while the house, if such it can be called would have contained more than one, perhaps two or three persons, the doorway could only have admitted one at a time, and the passage could easily have been defended by any one armed with a spear.

No Stone is mentioned. But there's plenty of evidence that the Nairne family, who owned the land including Dunsinnan, were searching the area busily – and that chambers or buildings were indeed hidden beneath its turfs. With such clear motivation to carry on digging on the part of the landowner, and if so much of the farm labourers' tale is true, why would the rest of it be false? And why have no academic papers so far discovered mentioned the Stone?

Archaeology began as a hobby for amateur historians, but it was not long before those interested wanted to turn it into an academic discipline in its own right. It therefore had to be developed along serious and scientific lines, in which idle speculation could not be allowed. Archaeologists then, as now, who want to be taken seriously, dare not risk their reputations by putting down in print mystic nonsense about disappearing rocks.

Victorian antiquarians continued to turn the site over. They left nothing written down, and none of their after-the-dig discussions have come down to us so far. Yet something sparked their curiosity. The state of their art was so crude that they ruined the site for further research, so that only now might those in the forefront of archaeology be able to learn anything new.

Dr Gregor Hutcheson, a retired geographer, using a life-time's professional knowledge of landscape and a set of dowsers' divining rods, hirples over the lumpy summit of Dunsinnan in deep fog, for a recent BBC film. We see the rods move and meet eerily, when he reaches the outer rampart of the fort. 'Divining rods provide a window on Scotland's past.' Dr Hutcheson shows us where the ground falls away, in what was obviously a landslip that happened – oh perhaps almost a hundred and eighty years ago? 'The Stone could well be somewhere in this vicinity,' he smiles.

The sheer number of digs undertaken proves Dunsinnan was attracting far greater interest than a small hill-fort would normally have merited, at a time when sites of major significance such as Scone and Forteviot were still untouched – indeed are still largely unexplored.

Who were these Nairnes? As custodians of Dunsinnan Hill they were guilty of quite some prodigality. They managed to lose not only the little ring, but also, it would appear, their unearthed Stone, after it had been safely hidden for centuries, so successfully that no trace of it remains. Their loss is symptomatic of their lack of regard for the artefacts of Scotland. And now they themselves have disappeared without trace. The Nairne family sold Dunsinnan Estate in 1898 and scattered from Africa to America. Glasgow journalist Margaret Wilson has long been fascinated by the Dunsinnan story and has worked for years trying to trace Nairne descendants because, she says, there must be papers, letters and records in existence of the activities of such an important Scottish family.

For a time Dunsinnan Estate belonged to the Bernard family,

Edinburgh brewers, then it came into the hands of the Sinclair family. It is now the property of Jamie Sinclair, the young Laird of Dunsinnan, whose grandfather devoted himself to understanding what the stories about the Stone all meant, and who says he was brought up to believe it might be hidden in the vicinity.

Meanwhile there has been controversy over the hill because a quarry at its base is threatening to gobble it up. The National Trust and other bodies have performed a holding operation whereby Macbeth's castle cannot be touched without their consent.

Ann and Peter Campbell are tenant farmers whose sheep roam Dunsinnan Hill. Ann, who has 'always known the real Stone of Destiny is hidden in a cave on the hill', gives her version of the story. 'The Monks of Scone Abbey are said to have put it there and gave King Edward I a replica ... A few years ago I read in the *Dundee Courier* that a gamekeeper was on the hill one day when there was a small landslide and he discovered a cave. Inside the cave he claims to have seen the "Stone", but by the time he went and got the laird and a few others another landslide had occurred and the cave had vanished.' She says 'the locals don't want to talk about it ... If you were to find out for definite there would be nothing left to dream on.'

The 1819 letter to *The Times* ended, tantalisingly, 'This curious stone has been shipped for London for the inspection of the scientific amateur, in order to discover its real quality.' So did the Stone, after all, end up in London?

A search was carried out in London during 1990 and it was learned that between 1817 and 1823 the Society of Antiquaries of London was the recipient of most newly discovered artefacts. Its members came from a wide variety of backgrounds, and the President – who chaired most of the meetings – happened to be a Scotsman, the Earl of Aberdeen. Many archaeological finds were discussed, occasionally of Scottish origin, but the Proceedings mention no large Stone, from Scotland or anywhere else. A search at the British Museum, repository of all earlier and smaller collections, with the help of Sue Youngs, Curator of Medieval and Later Antiquities, revealed nothing.

If the Stone had been 'shipped', it would be listed. The cargoes of all the ships arriving in the Thames were faithfully reported in the newspapers of the day. A careful scrutiny of these over a period of a year showed many cargoes arriving from Scotland, in ships which had suffered an interesting variety of accidents. No cargo included a Stone. This tallies with research done by McKerracher in Scotland, who checked reports of all ships sailing out of Perth over that period and found them empty of sizeable stones. Although 'shipped' might be considered a loose term also applied to the moving of freight on dry land, at that time Perth and the Tay, which is still navigable by sea-going boats, were by far the most feasible options for shipment of large and heavy objects. Unless and until further research shows otherwise, we can now be reasonably certain that wherever the Dunsinnan Stone went after mid-December 1818, it did not leave Scotland. It seems likely, therefore, that it will turn up in Perthshire.

There are a few more tantalising shreds of information. Lady Pamela Mansfield remembers hearing her father-in-law, the late Lord Mansfield, say the Stone had been 'carted away' from the site 'in the 1920s'. And D. M. Heyde, who once attempted to find the entrance to Dunsinnan fort, cites a local tradition that the Stone was taken 'in the first instance' to Bandirran, near Balbeggie – the village nearest to Dunsinnan Hill – though 'its subsequent disposal remains a mystery'.

In 1927, Dundee archaeologist Alexander Hutcheson, who seems to have got into the chamber on the hill himself in 1870, wrote that when Nairne's men discovered the underground chamber and the stone, they brought it down and carted it 'away'. He mentioned the two plaques and their inscription, giving his opinion that, while the place-name Bethel was not in doubt, the rest of the translation was probably not very good.

If Edward I was satisfied that he had found and taken the real Stone of Destiny in 1296, why had he then suddenly sent a raiding party of knights back to Scone on 17th August 1298, knights who ripped the Abbey apart in a desperate search for something? They returned to England empty-handed.

McKerracher goes on:

> The preliminary negotiations for the Treaty of Northampton in 1328 ... included the offer of the return of the Stone. Strangely, the Scots did not ask for the insertion of this clause in the formal document. Edward III offered to return it in 1328 and again in 1329, even suggesting the Queen Mother would take it personally to Berwick. It was offered a final time in 1363, but on none of these occasions do the Scots appear to have replied. So the sandstone block in London stayed where it was, and the real Stone ... was almost certainly hidden by Abbot Henry ... and as only a few senior monks would have known the location, it is likely this became lost through the passage of time. The Scots knew it was still within Scotland and thus made no effort to have the fake returned from London.

McKerracher's particular quest is for the plaques shown on the great seals of Malcolm V, Alexander I and David I. He cites the translation as an interesting clue, saying it must have been in Gaelic, in which language 'sconce' means 'protective shadow'.

Acair's 1989 Gaelic dictionary gives *faileas* for 'shadow' and *tearmunnach* for 'protective'. *Sgonnsa* is unequivocally given as 'fort'. Of course, over the centuries, in every language, words change meaning and connotation – perhaps the early Gaelic of mid-Perthshire mutated?

Meanwhile yet another tale comes in from a Perthshire electrician – he rather thinks he has seen an interesting-looking stone built into the basement of a Victorian house.

The Laird of Dunsinnan tells the truth when he remarks 'If we find the real Stone there will be such an enormous controversy. Everybody will be arguing about it and wanting to pinch a piece of 'the real thing'. If it did appear, would it be shipped off to Edinburgh? It's better left where it is.'

≈

CHAPTER NINETEEN

A ROYAL PECULIAR

For most people, however, the Stone that Edward I took to Westminster Abbey has always been regarded as the one and only Stone of Destiny. The curious Victorians died out, the twentieth century rolled on, and the Stone took its four-month trip to Scotland.

By the early 1950s King George VI was dead and his elder daughter Elizabeth crowned queen in his place, over whatever stone lay beneath the coronation chair, according to the English tradition described in Chapter 3. This meant that some of the fundamentals of the Scottish ceremony were left to be dealt with *ad hoc*, or omitted.

When Charles I came to the British throne in 1625, the first new king after the Union of Crowns in 1603, it was thought that he would come to Scotland for his coronation as King of Scots. Expected in 1626, he failed to show up; after costly preparations were put in hand in 1628 then again in 1631, he still didn't turn up. Finally, in June 1633, amid elaborate and excessive stage-management and heaps of seventeenth century kitsch, he arrived. He spent the night at Edinburgh Castle, then processed down the Royal Mile, the Honours of Scotland borne on a cushion before him by the most important in the land. In the Chapel Royal beside Holyrood House he was presented to his people, anointed king, mantled with the robe royal, and the crown was set on his head. Unfortunately it was not there for long. Not renowned for his tact on that occasion or any other, his ideas on church affairs in Scotland gave rise to the Covenanting movement, which affair led to his decapitation on the orders of Oliver Cromwell in 1649. Not a very promising precedent on which to build a new Scottish ceremony.

Wendy Wood, a passionate and irreverent Scottish Nationalist stirring in the 1950s, reminded us: 'The tradition of royalty in Scotland is different . . . Our kings were much closer to the people . . . The King of Scots was once the actual representative of the poor people by whom he could be approached at any time. James IV was the first Trade Unionist in that he worked incognito in the fields and after receiving his wage, sent word that in future payment must be higher. This is our natural tradition of royalty.'

When, therefore, it was announced that the Queen was to be known as Elizabeth II, many Scots objected, including Wood. While the coronation was going on at Westminster she was declaring to the public in Aberdeen: 'As you cannot have a second before a first (or there would be more claims for family allowances), Scotland is henceforth a republic.' The queen came on a State visit to Edinburgh in 1953. She was to receive the Scottish crown in St Giles Cathedral, Edinburgh. Wood describes the event: 'It was 131 years since The Honours of Scotland had been seen outside the walls of Edinburgh Castle, and the capital of Scotland was thrilled. But the occasion was obviously to be played down by the authorities from London. Court instruction implied that the peers were not expected to wear their robes . . . but to Scotland this was equivalent to the coronation in London.'

The Scottish dignitaries went ahead and wore the lot. Journalists described how

> Walter Elliot gleamed in the gold lace of a Privy Councillor. The bonnet feathers and bows of the Royal Archers, the peers in scarlet and ermine, the Countess of Errol in her crimson robe, all was splendid and full of colour . . . But the Queen? She was in a plain blue shopping dress; it seemed like a slap in the face for the nation. The Very Revd Charles Warr, who received Her Majesty at the door, looked as if he were going to faint from shock . . . At the great moment in St Giles when the Duke of Hamilton presented Scotland's Crown to Her Majesty, the Queen stretched out her hand with her bag

dangling from her arm! It seemed like a deliberate insult to Scotland and the offending object had to be painted over in the official recording of the event.

Wood was further stunned when, on the queeen's visit to New Zealand 'where she styled herself on the radio as "Queen of England", the Maoris were honoured with the real coronation robe.' Gleefully Wood noted that this blunder gave rise to a court case in which two Scottish sisters refused to pay their income tax to the English Treasury on the legal premise that Her Majesty's reference to herself on a world-wide broadcast as the 'Queen of England' presupposed two different kingdoms and they were only prepared to pay their tax to the Scottish one.

So disgusted was Wood with the insensitive behaviour of the English Court that every pinprick became unbearable. When, in 1962, King Olaf of Norway came to visit Edinburgh, an EIIR sign was reported on the North Bridge. 'The sign was on a shield about twenty-five feet up on a lamp-post – a puzzle to get at. It could not at that height be painted out or removed. So I blew three eggs, filled them with waterproof ink, coloured purple, red and black, plugged the holes with plasticine and going to the bridge in the evening, hurled the first egg at the target. It skiffed the side of the board and dived into the street below, with what possible result I shuddered to think. The second egg and the third hit the target, and I felt that having played cricket at school had not been wasted after all. I was on my way home when a reluctant policeman invited me into his box . . . Denial was useless with hands so stained that all the detergents of Leverhulme would not cleanse them.'

In many another country this rebel would have thrown a bomb and started a civil war. Perhaps the Scots' fondness for defusing situations with ridicule is one of their more useful traits.

Yet the frustration continued. Some of it focused on the Coronation Stone. Who legally owned it? Did it belong to the Crown, the State, the Church? The question of ownership had been argued off and on since the time of Edward I. Because he had made an offering of it to St Edward when he got it to Westminster, the abbots regarded it as the property, not of the Crown, but of the saint and hence the Church. However the presence of leopards in the decoration of the Coronation Chair shows that Edward thought of the Stone as royal property. So when it was due to be handed back to the Scots in 1328, the Throne and the Church had a difference of opinion. The Chronicle of Lanercost says the abbot refused to let it go, and the Londoners, who saw it as a legitimate trophy of war symbolising the overthrow of the Scottish kingdom, agreed with him. The answer perhaps lies somewhere among the convoluted principles of English and Scots law which, as we have seen, differ fundamentally from each other. But the question has never been tested in court.

Now, we are informed as the Stone comes back to Scotland on loan, it belongs to the Crown.

What if an original Stone of Destiny should be found in Scotland? Would Scotland Yard – or the British Museum – come and snatch it away? Or would it belong where it was found? For precedent one only has to look at the Chess Men of Lewis. Perhaps it would be cut up and apportioned? And if, as seems quite likely, the Stone presently on loan in Edinburgh Castle was never used in a Scottish king-making ceremony, was never the pillow of either St Columba or Jacob, what claim can the Scottish people possibly have on it? That, having been dug from a Perthshire quarry, it was a piece of absentee land?

If Edward's Stone was replaced by a Bertie Gray joke facsimile in 1951, does it not legally belong to his estate – perhaps to his grand-niece Katy? It would make a fitting tombstone for Gray, put a suitable lid on all the doubts he so enjoyed engendering.

Why have these questions never been discussed thoroughly in a court of law? Could it be that the complexities of establishing ownership of the Westminster stone were beyond the greatest legal brains in England? Was this why the actions of the

English authorities, in both 1296 and 1951, were to grab the Stone, secure it, and only then promise discussion, maybe, someday?

Kay Matheson, Ian Hamilton, Gavin Vernon, Alan Stuart and their accomplices and sympathisers clearly believed the Westminster Stone belonged to the Scottish people. After all, treaty after treaty with England since 1296 had promised the return of their property.

But, even after Westminster got a stone back that April day in 1951, the question was not resolved. For some reason charges were not pressed. Since then, Hamilton has confessed all in his books, yet no charges were laid, no prosecutions took place and the young reivers were not brought to 'justice'. No satisfactory explanations were ever given to the public about the reasons for this waiving of the normal formalities. The truth was that unless ownership could be proved, Westminster would have had no case.

It was in an attempt to force open discussion on the ownership question that David Stewart, a twenty-four-year-old English-born Scotsman, decided to make his own bid for the Stone in August 1974. Talking fast and emphatically, Stewart explains how, from an early age he had been 'very heavily into politics'. A General Election was due and he wanted to keep the question of nationalism in the front of people's minds. 'It's always been very difficult to get the Scottish people moving.'

He laid his plans. When he arrived at Westminster Abbey luck appeared to be with him: renovation was going on and all the steps were ramped; the builders themselves had been moving huge stones around. The Coronation Chair was surrounded by spiked railings, apparently of wrought iron and there was no gate. How could he get in? Using logic – it was clean, therefore cleaners got in, therefore there was a secret opening – and with his minute observation – he was a trained geologist-archaeologist – he noticed a loose spike. 'You can lift it off, and then push the railings in.

There's no alarm on the railings.' He worked out how the seat came apart.

He went home to Wolverhampton, made a collapsible trolley, a harness, a ramp for his mini, and packed the pieces into two large shopping bags.

The Abbey opened late on Wednesdays. The car park for the Houses of Parliament was open all night just across the road. 'Things were conspiring in my favour, quite honestly, so I felt pressurised to do it.' On the night of 4th September 1974 he drove south.

He had two plans: either to get the Stone away north to Scotland, or, if he should be caught, to be brought to court accused of theft. Either way, ownership would have to be tried.

The IRA then 'decided to blow up the Houses of Parliament. They planted a bomb in the cafeteria. So the place was absolutely solid with guards.' But Stewart decided to go ahead. Held up by traffic, he was late getting into the Abbey. Wandering casually in amongst the last visitors, 'the cable around my body, two enormous carrier bags, and a camera round my neck to look like a tourist,' he suddenly realised he had left his tools in the car.

'I thought – it can't be done. But I've written a letter to the press telling them about this. It's got to be done.' He retrieved them at the run, and re-entered the Abbey just as people were being ushered out. He stopped a guard. 'And because his job was to show people where things were he pointed the way. He hid under an altar till the Abbey shut at eight o'clock. A guard walked round. An hour and a half later came another. 'And that was it. The place was my own.

'I was going to wait till two a.m., but I got so bored. I got inside the railings, saw four pressure alarms underneath each corner. If you moved the Stone at all you would set it off. Sometimes you've just got to take a chance. I thought – the alarm may not actually work. There was this gigantic thick five-core wire. I cut through it. Nothing happened.'

He dismantled the Chair and strung his cable to the railings. Tipping the Chair forward he let the Stone fall into the sling. 'It went down with one hell of a crash, just missed my legs. I hadn't realised just how big it was. That was when I found out the railings were not wrought iron they were cast iron. One of these big pineapple jobs with the cord round it snapped, whistled over my head at the speed of light and thumped into the tomb of Edward the Confessor. The Stone dropped slam onto the trolley and flattened the front wheels splat. The noise was like the crack of doom – the whole Abbey reverberated. But no-one came.

'I was getting it out, when I heard the police sirens. It's the strangest feeling when you know they're coming for *you*.

'Three or four minutes after, the doors opened and the lights came on. They'd never been in the place in their lives – they didn't know where the Stone was. Somebody turned up eventually, flashed his torch on me – then went away again. A minute later they turned up in force and that was that.

'They wanted to know where all my mates were. It takes six to move the Stone.

'I was heaved into Brixton prison for a week. Very educational. I'd recommend it to anyone. Very bizarre place. I was charged with theft immediately.

'They give you a copy of the charge-sheet. I was charged with attempting to steal a Stone which was the property of the Dean and Chapter of Westminster.

'Somebody must have realised what the charge implied. I was out doing the rounds of the exercise yard, and someone went through my clothes where the charge sheet was, and took it. Twenty minutes before I was due to appear in Court they told me the charge of theft was dropped.'

Six weeks later, after the General Election, on 22nd October 1974 at Bow Street, Magistrate Evelyn Russell conditionally discharged him, ordering him to pay £150 damages, and £75 costs. A police witness reported that on being apprehended

Stewart had said 'How can I steal something that is already stolen?'

How did he feel? 'Relieved. I'm not a violent man. It was a symbolic gesture.'

In 1977 Stewart stood for Newington Council in Edinburgh. Having invested twelve years in the SNP, he wanted to stay in Scottish politics. For him 'the 1979 Referendum was a knife in the heart. It demoralised everybody. If the Scots weren't interested then I felt I wasn't prepared to keep bashing my head against a brick wall indefinitely. So I left and just got on with my job.' He now works as a respectable on-site archaeologist for the Scottish Office, sometimes with Dr Caldwell of the Finlaggan Trust. 'Almost certainly the real Stone of Destiny never went south. Because as David Caldwell says – and he's a man who knows his history of Scotland – the Scots never asked for it back. And this was one of their most precious things, their Kingship Stone. So it cannot have been the real one. I'm convinced it's around. But I don't think anyone's keeping it. Because, if they were, they would have used the opportunity sometime in the recent past of saying "we've got the real one". I keep looking for it. I go digging sites all over Scotland – all archaeologists keep a weather eye out for it, but they're reticent – everyone's looking after their reputations. This is political, and they will take no risks.

'Someone's going to turn it up. It's got to be here. It will be recognisable – it's an important stone and it will have been worked.' He calls the Stone in Edinburgh, 'a really scabby piece of garbage, a random block'.

What if Stewart, or anyone else, should dig up the Stone of Destiny somewhere in Scotland? Legally, all ancient objects discovered in Scotland, whether or not they have intrinsic value, belong first to the Crown. 'The finder receives its market value, and possibly that of any treasure trove subsequently found on the site, and your find may be returned to you. In this way the accidental finder can't lose.'

Of course one of the problems is recognition that you've

found something of special interest. Nowadays we view with horror the builders of Arthurstone House in Perthshire who, two hundred years ago, blew up Arthur's Stone for building materials. Some time after this Dunsinnan House was also built. But could the farmer in upper Clydesdale who recently bulldozed away the centre of the ancient motte near his farm-steading, for a handy silage pit, be blamed? In Scots law, ignorance is not regarded as an excuse.

At present, says an eminent Scottish QC working in London, there remains the question of whether ownership would be settled by English or Scots law. In England, unless anyone can prove a contrary title, ownership is vested in the Crown.

In 1991 Richard Mortimer, Archivist at Westminster Abbey, kindly replied to an enquiry. 'Experience suggests that the Church rarely speaks with a single voice' but 'it seems clear that its significance is monarchic rather than religious . . . The Stone legally belongs to the Dean and Chapter of Westminster. The Abbey is a "Royal Peculiar" and comes directly under the Queen, on whose behalf the Dean and Chapter administer the Abbey.'

Who are we to argue with such a statement? We may have been the defrauded owners of an ancient relic – or Westminster may have been the deluded possessors of a cesspit lid. Meanwhile amateur Stone-seekers are free to look for alternative pieces of rock-art around the bogs, hills, castles and islands of Scotland.

CHAPTER TWENTY

————————— ≈ —————————

BACK TO THE FUTURE

On Wednesday 3rd July 1996, the Secretary of State for Scotland announced out of the blue that the Coronation Stone was to be returned. The news came through to the Press at lunchtime, and by three o'clock the House of Commons was reeling in its seats as MPs were given the news.

Michael Forsyth told reporters that since he was a schoolboy of seven he had believed the Stone should be in Scotland, but the idea is said to have been reinforced by his ten-year-old daughter Katie.

A bemused and unprepared Scotland did not know how to react. As we have seen in Chapters 2 and 3, discussion about the Stone of Scone had continued almost unbroken for forty-five years – the BBC even made a little film-noir about the 1950 affair entitled 'The Pinch'. John Rollo had died and his secret recording became available for broadcast. Dozens of Letters to Editors had been penned. But in July 1996, the response from ordinary Scots to Forsyth's coup was curiously flat.

It did, however, spark off reaction in the media. Dorothy Grace-Elder roundly told her readers that, since the Stone was only a 'Lavvy Lid', the Scone cesspit cover, they should concentrate on more important issues.

The general feeling was one of deep distrust. People tried to work out Forsyth's motives, unable to believe this politician could simply be completing Edward I's 'unfinished business' – he must be doing something nasty behind all these headlines. Returning a 'bauble' associated with monarchical power to a disenfranchised nation was seen as a cynical act of political opportunism.

Laughter-mongers got busy; Edward I was resuscitated from

the grave to remind political rulers of the lurking Scottish 'banana skins' that had previously unseated them. Radio Borders burst into song suggesting Forsyth should end up in the river Tweed 'wi the stane roond his neck'. A cartoonist proposed using it as a Glasgow wheel-clamp, or a satellite entitled '2001 + A Scottish Oddyssey'. His paper good humouredly offered to return gifts to the English, starting with absentee landlords, the *Sun* newspaper, redundant nuclear submarines, and tripe.

Newspapers were inundated with letters. Was the government asset-stripping: would the return of the Stone be followed by the repatriation of Cleopatra's Needle, the Elgin Marbles, and the Rock of Gibraltar? The Stone was receiving far more coverage than the burning issues of the day.

Where should the returning Stone go? Dunadd, ancient capital of Dalriada, Dunfermline Abbey to honour the bones of Bruce; Scone whence it had come; Stirling Castle; a spot equidistant from four pubs in Elderslie for Wallace's memory; St Giles Cathedral – because the church needed something to draw the crowds? Professor Christopher Smout, Historiographer Royal, touted the new Museum of Scotland. But no sooner was a resting place proposed than objections were raised to it.

Scone wouldn't do; in 1296 the Church had owned the land of what was now the Palace and its estate, at present merely a tourist attraction where there existed no secure resting place for the Stone – and anyway the Scottish people should not have to pay tourist fees to see what belonged to them; Edinburgh Castle already had more than its fair share of tourist money. North Tayside MP Bill Walker suddenly promised a purpose-built 'Kingship Centre' at Scone. Robbie the Pict suggested Leac Trotternish, Skye. Someone decided it should go back to Ireland since it came from the Lia Fail at Tara. Another correspondent wanted the ex-pillow to be returned to Jacob's homeland, Israel, whilst a Plockton peacemaker had the idea of putting a replica stone in each of the locations with a claim to it.

All through the debate, an old man smiled. The Revd John Mackay Nimmo, Keeper of the Stone of Destiny for the Knights Templar, was certain that they had the real thing. He didn't care if it rained stones, what mattered was that Scotland should have a parliament of its own, whose Speaker should sit on their one. He died shortly before the Westminster Stone returned, but not before several correspondents and politicians publicly agreed with him that the most fitting place for it would indeed be in a new Scottish Parliament.

On 16th July six volumes of documents, till then classified and secret, were opened at the General Registrar's Office in Edinburgh, in the hope of quelling any remaining suspicions that the Coronation Stone was not the genuine article taken by Edward I – suspicions left, it has to be said, by the redoubtable Bertie Gray who appears to have made several death-bed speeches about which stone was what. Indeed there had been so many stones that he couldn't actually remember whether the one he had fixed up was the one that had been left in Arbroath Abbey that April day – or not.

'Ham's Homepage' popped up on the Internet, headed 'The Stone of Destiny'. It reminded surfers how 'patriotic students' succeeded in a 'daring raid to recapture the Stone' and asked 'Is this the real Stone?', inviting comments to Hamish@rmplc.co.uk.

Throughout the summer holidays the debate grumbled on. Edinburgh and Leith Conservative Association said it should remain at Westminster. Other Scots wanted it back. They thought it should be a rolling stone, it should go to the New Arlington Bar in Glasgow because it had rested there in 1950–51. A System Three poll commissioned by Perthshire Tourist Board found 55 per cent of Scots plumped for Scone, 25 per cent for Edinburgh, 5 per cent Stirling, 2 per cent each for Perth, Iona and Dunfermline, 1 per cent for Arbroath and fewer for Dunadd. However a government consultation exercise eliciting 'about eighty responses' mainly from churches, MPs, councils and 'titled individuals', opted for Edinburgh Castle. Cynics said the Stone should be stuffed with the heart of Bruce and a portrait of Bonnie Prince Charlie, wrapped in the Declaration of Arbroath and some tartan, and either hurled into Loch Ness to brain the monster, or dropped from a great height on the statue of the Duke of Sutherland.

The Scottish Office replied politely to a letter from Robbie the Pict; the Stone remains the property of the Crown and, while it would be housed in Scotland, it would be taken back to Westminster for future coronations.

Ian Hamilton QC (seventy-one), presently Rector of Aberdeen University, took up the issue of the monarchy. Speaking as one of the 'ordinary people of Scotland' who had a 'fierce pride' in his leaderless nation, he invited 'Betty Windsor' not to accompany this piece of 'meaningless masonry' north, saying 'we are no longer ruled by sovereigns. Sovereignty now rests with the Scottish people.'

Dr Sandy Grant, Reader in Mediaeval History at Lancaster University, warned 'Returning it now in place of self-government could boost nationalist passions. Forsyth is playing with fire.'

In October the very rock beneath Edinburgh began to shudder. Was it troubled by the notion of this hunk of Perthshire Stone invading its territory? Between the 2nd and the 30th, thirty-four earthquakes shook the teacups of Morningside, rattled the glasses in the bars of the Grassmarket and generally caused siesmographic wobbles. What would happen when that slice of Scone actually hit the city?

The date of the 'Shortbread parade' was set for St Andrew's Day, 30th November, but the controversy raged on. What about the manner of its arrival? Gretna, 'Gateway to Scotland', wanted to grab it as it crossed the Border, but so did Langholm, and Annan in recognition of the number of times it was burned down by English armies, and Dumfries. The little town of Coldstream won, because Edward I had 'swaggered' through it with the Stone, crossing the River Tweed by its ford, on his way south in 1296. Coldstream also commemorated the nearby Battle of Flodden (1513).

Headline writers scraped together the last of their puns; 'Stone conspirators reunited with old quarry', 'Borders battle over Stone's Scottish Tour', 'Scots get the Scone, but Major wants the jam'.

And what about English reaction? After all, Westminster Abbey was not in the habit of losing relics. The Dean, the Very Reverend Michael Mayne, and his Chapter, were said to be 'deeply annoyed', insisting that the Stone 'should not be regarded as a secular museum piece', but that its religious associations should be respected.

However, in the darkness of dawn on 14th November 1996 at 7 a.m., four stalwart men staggered from a back entrance of Westminster Abbey bearing the Stone, boxed in blue metal, stamped with a red wax seal. The scene was witnessed by a handful of sleepy journalists and photographers. One reporter summed up the scene in a word: underwhelming.

The Dean felt as if he had lost a member of his family, saying that the whole of the Westminster community felt bereaved. Columnist Brian Sewell called the removal of the Stone from its chair 'an act of indefensible vandalism'. A tourist queried, 'Why on earth do they want it back?'

After an overnight stop under armed guard, and total media blackout, at Albemarle Barracks, near Newcastle-upon-Tyne, the Stone of Scone was driven north.

The people of Coldstream did not appear to be losing any sleep over the media spotlight beaming in on their town, though they had strung 400 yards of street with red white and blue flags, from the Toon Heid Chippie to the Tourist Information Centre. The town had been closed to the public since early morning. Sniffer dogs, Special Branch officers and boat patrols combed the area.

Media folk gathered around the end of the town, where the five-arch bridge takes traffic across the border to England.

By ten, a few Coldstream citizens, individuals from Aberdeen, Glasgow and London, Welsh Nationalists and an Australian television team, had joined them to form a small crowd headed by 158 local schoolchildren waving home-made Saltires. The Coldstream Guards marched in with their pipers, to man the bridge. Twelve Scottish Nationalists from Dundee, who disapproved of 'the enormous waste of public money', were foiled in their attempt to disrupt proceedings with a loud-hailer.

Otherwise the scene was peaceful enough. Beyond, a farmer carried on ploughing his English acres. A watery sun shone between strips of cloud, gleaming on the broad stretch of river where a salmon fisherman cast his line from a boat kept steady in the flow by his oarsman. His dog looked on. A few bored schoolboys kicked their football into the water. Police divers rescued it.

A black bomber roared in from the east, then another. A ceremonial fly-past? No – this was a low flying practice area. Planes continued to hurtle up and down the river for the rest of the morning. Wasn't the RAF briefed? A helicopter approached, hovered, and sank to the ground out of sight in England. It was now half-past ten.

A rumour wafted through the waiting crowd like the wind through barley – delay of some kind, trouble with English protesters, a bomb scare. Eventually the Bomb Disposal team's white van crept gingerly onto the bridge. A shoe box was retrieved.

Soldiers were planted at regular intervals. The helicopter rose to hover above the river and, an hour late, shortly after 11 a.m., a small motorcade hove into sight. At that moment a finger of sunlight shone down, illuminating five swans swooping downstream, their wings lit gold and silver.

Two closed landrovers sandwiching a white transit van made their way to the exact centre of the bridge, where a plaque commemorates the moment in 1787 when Robert Burns crossed the border to England.

There the vehicles were handed over amid much slapping

of guns, stamping of boots, yelling of commands, and the shaking of hands on the part of grey-suited individuals as an inaudible ceremony took place. The pipes and drums struck up 'The Return of the Stone' (newly composed by Captain Gavin Stoddart, Director of Army Bagpipe Music at Edinburgh Castle), and the little cavalcade inched on to Scottish soil, seven hundred and a quarter years after it had passed in the opposite direction beneath, also under armed guard.

A single shout rang from the hillside above the bridge. 'Freedom!'

The crowd looked a mite embarrassed at such a display of emotion, and remained almost silent as the anonymous vehicles purred by. The cargo might as well have been a crate of Newcastle coals. 'I really wanted to see what it looked like,' said thirteen-year-old Markus Pilgram.

At Coldstream town centre the politicians celebrated with a dram, and a sound-bite or two, in civilised fashion. Secretary of State Michael Forsyth re-ran his 'unfinished business' speech, Labour's Shadow Secretary of State George Robertson did his 'we want the substance not the symbol' number, then they and other officials met with Major-General Sir John Swinton, Lord Lieutenant of Berwickshire. At no point did the subject of the little celebration make an appearance.

How much better it would have been if the Stone had been borne across the bridge open to the skies, for all to see. No one in Coldstream could understand the reason for secrecy. After all, our Stone was now on friendly territory.

Before the morning was over, new conspiracy theories were sprouting like winter wheat. Popping into the Green Shutters tearoom for a heat and 'Stone Specials' of coffee and 'Scones', we heard the whispers: the Stone had been taken to Edinburgh secretly weeks ago; the Landrovers were empty – three big soldiers had leapt into one, but there wouldn't have been room for them if the Stone had truly been there. Mrs Bloggs had got a look in – and sure enough there was nothing to see. It was all a con dreamed up by Westminster in general and 'wee Forsyth' in particular, for nefarious, unmentionable and definitely suspect reasons of their own.

In no time the motorcade rolled out of town on its way to the Gyle laboratories of Historic Scotland, near Edinburgh, where it was to undergo 'restoration' to prepare it for exhibition alongside the Honours of Scotland. Vital statistics given to the public veered crazily – it weighed 350lbs, no, 410lbs, that is 800lbs – er – about the same weight as an MP.

Two weeks went by. Robertson warned Forsyth that he'd opened a Pandora's Box: 'The danger for Tories is that they are exciting the sense of Scottish nationhood without offering anything to the nation itself.' Scots were reminded by columnist Angus Peter Campbell how entire kingdoms had been exchanged for chunks of coloured glass, how generations of Scottish people had been persuaded that their clothing, their culture, their language were worthless and should be traded in for the 'polished beads of the English' till all they could see in the mirror was a reflection of what the English had persuaded them they were.

One Londoner declared 'It's diabolical. The Scots are all so greedy.' Professor George Henderson, expert on medieval art, newly retired from Cambridge University, and his wife Dr Isobel Henderson, leading authority on the Picts, wrote to *The Times*. They felt very strongly about the Stone's 'naked' future. Stripped from its historical context, which had symbolised not subjugation but the Union of the Scottish and English Crowns, it had lost a setting of 'transcendental beauty and decorum'. The old 'Thunderer' dutifully published one or two dignified articles before falling silent. The English people had already lost interest in the Stone.

Then Virginia Wills of Bridge-of-Allan began to ask questions about the Coronation Chair. The National Library of Scotland agreed that new research seemed to suggest it had been made in Scotland and also stolen by Edward I. Emotional pleas were lodged demanding the chair's return. In front of our eyes, a new sport of the Stone legend was alive and well and growing in Scotland.

Commerce seized the opportunity to climb on the Stone's back. Biggar businessman Arthur Bell, Chair of the Scottish Tory Reform Group, launched a new Speyside single malt whisky to commemorate the return of the Stone, *Dram of Destiny*. Only 2,500 bottles would be issued, at £24.95 each, and Bell was confident that the many malt collectors in England would want to invest in a few.

On 27th November Michael Bruce Forsyth was elected *Spectator* magazine's 'Parliamentarian of the Year'. *Herald* readers were informed that he saw himself as 'a modern-day Marquis of Montrose'. The Tories' poll in Scotland remained at or below 13 per cent.

Preparations for the big day were in hand. Dwellers on the Royal Mile were being rudely awakened early in the morning while practice parades were held.

On the evening of 29th November the Nationalists held a torchlit procession, pre-empting the celebrations with their 'Freedom March.' Dorothy-Grace Elder told movingly how Kay Matheson, 'a heroic daughter of Scotland, once a Braveheart outlaw whom a furious king ordered to be hunted down' stood quietly while 'the cheers of hundreds thundered and crashed around her.'

Then, lit by a cold sun, Scotland's National Day began. The 30th November, St Andrew's Day, inspires celebrations of varying intensity. In this particular year, *Tones of Destiny, Chapman* magazine's festival of twenty-five years of existence, intended to mark the eighty-fifth birthday of the Gaelic poet Sorley MacLean, had sadly been turned into his wake. George Wyllie was unveiling his new *Destiny Installation*.

Neither of these involved quite the complexity of preparation promulgated for the Stone. The Lyon Clerk, Ms Elizabeth Roads, explained how, after much research, experts in protocol had decided the event should be much like one accorded to a visiting Head of State; grander than the opening of the

General Assembly of the Church of Scotland, less grand than the Queen's coronation.

Accordingly, Saturday television schedules, from budget responses to football fixtures, were telescoped to provide space for an on-the-spot *Return of the Stone*, with highlights at night; a documentary made for the BBC Arts series Ex-S: *The Stone of Destiny*; and a re-run of *The Pinch*. The Stone would be guarded by 1,200 service personnel. Prince Andrew, representing the Queen, would do the official hand-over at the Castle. A twenty-one-gun salute would be fired, to which HMS *Newcastle*, near Leith, would reply. A thousand guests had been invited, including celebrities such as *Braveheart*'s Mel Gibson, and old 007 himself – Sean Connery; ex Rugby Captain Gavin Hastings, football hero Allie McCoist, actor Robbie Coltrane, and of course the four people who had brought the Stone back in 1950. Ten schoolchildren from all over Scotland would take part in the service at St Giles Cathedral, and £50,000 was to be spent on the ceremony.

With a clean bill of health from Graeme Munro, in spite of its 1951 repair having been 'relatively crude', the Stone was cleaned up and set in its specially lit perspex display cabinet, this time on an open landrover, ready to greet its subjects.

Protected by eight members of the Royal Company of Archers, a Royal Mile of servicemen and women standing a measured six metres apart with bayonets fixed, countless police and security men and three glamorous fellows on pretty grey horses, the Stone set out on its apparently dangerous journey through the gates of Holyrood Palace, to the tune of *Mission Impossible* played by the Royal Marines. A handful of onlookers stood pressed like cattle behind seamless lines of crush barriers. Security chiefs had dictated that strictly no procession would be permitted to form behind the Stone.

Hefted nervously up the steps of the East (back) door of St Giles by ten soldiers, into the Sanctuary where it remained invisible to most of the congregation, the Stone was played to, sung to, read to, spoken about and welcomed home by the Moderator of the Church of Scotland the Rt Rev John McIndoe. But even if choirs of angels themselves had appeared, the Stone could not have responded. For it was not a Head of State. It was not animate. It simply lay there on its bier like a lump of cold porridge, or a stale scone, or even a cut block of sandstone petrified in an ancient sea waiting to be built into something beautiful.

The doughy accoustic of St Giles soaked up Benjamin Britten, Henry Purcell and chanted litanies. Mercifully the readings sandwiched between these came in the three languages of Scotland: English spoken with a Scottish accent, the Doric, and Jacob's Dream sounding like a poem by Sorley MacLean himself in Gaelic.

Meanwhile Canon Kenyon Wright, Chairman of the Scottish Constitutional Convention, planted a rowan tree in the grounds of the future parliament building. 'Planting a tree shows our faith in the future of Scotland.'

Kay Matheson, wrapped in soft green tartan, joined in the ceremony with obvious delight. 'It was all worth it. It wasn't as strenous as last time – we didn't have the Army to help us.' Gavin Vernon flew in from Canada 'the adrenalin running through my veins'; Alan Stuart 'never thought it would come to anything like this', feeling that Michael Forsyth had 'made a better job of getting it back' and that he was 'very happy to see the stone again'. Ian Hamilton refused to attend the 'charade' although pleased his action was being honoured during his lifetime.

After the St Giles ceremony, the Stone was carried out of the East Door and slid back onto its 'Stonemobile'. Sheepishly following a sinister-looking line of black limos filled with 'the anglicised aristocracy of Scotland, Commissioners of Regalia, Kings at Arms, Captains General and Gold Sticks', it crept up the High Street to the Castle. The atmosphere provided by the protocol artists had turned out to be that of a state funeral.

When the Royal Marines in their pith helmets squinted down their tubas and played God Save the Queen for Prince Andrew and Michael Forsyth, several people booed. Banners spelled out messages that the bread of democracy could not be replaced by stone. They were held by lookalikes from *Braveheart* battle scenes such as John Orr of the Vigil for Democracy, which had by then slept rough at the foot of Calton Hill for 1,694 nights. When the four Tornadoes screamed overhead on their official fly-past they set off shop alarms in the High Street. Down in the New Town, pavements bulged with Christmas shoppers bent on a bargain, oblivious to what was going on above their heads.

The High Street crowd, estimated at between 10,000 and 12,000, remained strangely silent as their Stone passed by. There was a sense of culture-clash, a failure of communication, an emptiness and anti-climax, along with a definite dash of hostility. What exactly had that display of military strength been designed to suggest?

Asked for their opinions, onlookers were torn: 'Does modern-day Scotland actually *need* someone called Gold Stick?' It had been a dead day for a dead nation which had a lump of symbolic rock less authentic than a Pot Noodle where its heart should be. The ceremony had nothing to do with the dignity of a country which wanted to look after its own affairs. A placard read '*The Stone of Questiony*'. One small boy was disappointed: 'Is *that* the Stone of Disney?'; another remarked, 'It's awful wee, isn't it?'

People found it difficult to express how they felt – certainly not grateful for the return of stolen property, certainly affronted at the notion it is only on loan, hoping it would be the first in a long line of other things Scots had lost being reclaimed, such as the Book of Deer, the Lewis Chessmen – and whatever they each understood as freedom. Many felt ambivalent about the Stone's obvious lack of glamour, and vaguely uncomfortable; had they been persuaded to come out and admire the Emperor's New Clothes? They found it impossible to believe that such an insignificant object could ever have been worthy of serious attention. This could only be a spoof. They objected to a ceremony they saw as blatant colonialism – all these bared bayonets suggesting that if ordinary Scottish people should dare to deviate from the given British system, break ranks and dance up the Royal Mile cheering the Stone and singing the 'Freedom Come-All-Ye' they would be gralloched on the spot for insurrection.

Placed on a crimson dais in the Great Hall at the top of the Castle, surrounded by ropes and tassels, the stone was attended by two bearskinned scarlet-jacketed soldiers and a small proportion of the 800 guests who had turned up. Prince Andrew alias the Earl of Inverness handed over the Stone officially to the Commissioners of the Regalia, and to a kilted Michael Forsyth, Keeper of the Great Seal, who had to promise to return it to Westminster when required. He practically curtsied.

Perhaps the only truly moving moment of that day came when protocol at last broke down. Apart from a happy Michael Forsyth, enjoying his moment, most of the officals had gone home for tea by the time a few parents brought their children in to take a look at the Stone. Clearly believing in its enchantment, a little girl dressed in red, Caroline Pringle, asked if she could touch the Stone. Forsyth lifted the barrier rope himself and, taking the photo-opportunity as his due, helped her up the steps to lay her hand on it. One by one the other children went reverently to place their hands on the Stone, lending their magic to it, until the security men noticed, and clamped down on them.

Permitted to view it a few days later, tourists who came to see the Crown Jewels were perplexed. Why had some numpty dumped this lump of sandstone rubble in their showcase? No placard offered an explanation. The knowledgeable were imbued with a sense of embarrassment.

The real Duke of Montrose penned a letter to the *Herald* upbraiding his 'whingeing Jocks' for not thanking the Queen 'for allowing its return', eliciting one response that a reader had been 'repelled by the pantomime' in which, though we had asked for a parliament, we were given a stone. Another threatened that though nowadays Forsyth was unlikely to lose his head, his seat was a different matter.

With time to reflect, calm observers agreed that Forsyth had pulled off quite a clever stunt and yes, it was nice to have the Stone of Scone back, but what problems had it solved? Scots didn't worship stones any more. Some hoped it might prove inspirational for Scotland's future.

It may all end in Hollywood. At least two films are currently planned, starring the Stone of Scone which will play the part of the Stone of Destiny.

≈

CHAPTER TWENTY-ONE

THE STONE OF DESTINY

If it is true that somewhere in Scotland an old Stone of Destiny exists, then at some point it will turn up. It lies either deliberately hidden underground or underwater, accidentally forgotten, or broken into pieces. How will it be identified?

Most experts interested in an original Stone now agree that the one described in early writings and shown on old seals was considerably larger than the Stone of Scone. The references to 'marble', 'hieroglyphics' and 'hollows' strongly suggest it was made of very hard shiny stone, and decorated or inscribed in some way. We are also told it stood on legs.

The Stone of Destiny was credited with having magic powers. It was said to shout with glee when the true monarch was inaugurated on it. In the late twentieth century we are still attempting to pacify pagan forces – by crossing our fingers to ward off the evil eye, touching wood for luck, and hanging pieces of our clothing on trees near 'cloutie' wells to leave difficulties behind with them. We may not believe deeply in superstitions – but we like to err on the safe side.

What would an original Stone look like? It was used in Christian times, as we know, therefore it is likely to be carved with a blend of Christian and pagan symbols – a cross perhaps, and spirals for sun-worship. There could be Pictish pictures like the boar, Irish emblems like the harp, even some evidence of Anglo-Saxon influence. We know the sort of designs that would have been used, for then, as now, there was a to and fro of artistic ideas from one medium to another; for instance, Susan Youngs, Curator of Medieval and Later Antiquities at the British Museum, London, traces how the fine designs drawn by Irish and Scottish monastic illuminators inspired gold and silversmiths. Columba and Irish contemporaries produced beautifully illuminated gospels like the *Book of Durrow* and the *Book of Kells*, and it is clear that one of their inspirations was the fine metalwork of the day. The ancestor of a Lindisfarne animal scroll is found on a bowl at Sutton Hoo in Suffolk. The idea of animal ornament probably came from Roman metalworkers. Bede mentioned metalwork being brought in by Anglo-Saxon travellers, and through Dal Riada came Germanic designs and forms in the seventh century, on the evidence of Dunadd – a centre of fine metalwork, such as bird-headed brooches. Other finds at Craig Phadrig, near Inverness, show similar influences. Pictish stone-workers also found inspiration in these things, and we see the results scattered about Scotland from Sueno's Stone near Findhorn on the Moray Firth to the Latinus Stone at Whithorn, with a particularly rich collection in the triangle between Arbroath, Montrose and Meigle. With that amount of artistic precedent, and the stone-carving skills available at every stage of the Stone's story, there is no reason to think it would be anything other than a most beautifully decorated artefact.

Norman Atkinson, Head of Support Services in the Cultural Services Department of Angus Council, and till recently Curator of Montrose Museum, is certain that the hollow described on top of the Stone is a footprint, because the custom of standing in the previous king's footprint was such a central feature of the early inauguration ceremonies. The boar was a symbol of Pictish royalty – the one at Dunadd could not have been put there by a Dalriadic Scot, therefore it is more likely that it was the 'stamp' of Angus I, a Pict who must have been there by agreement because the boar was never later removed or defaced.

Celtic peoples have always loved bright colours. There is the artistry of their illustrated manuscripts, and we can still see their painted carvings in some medieval churches. It is almost beyond doubt that such a revered object as the Stone of Destiny would not only have been elaborately carved, but also painted. The sort of colours and designs used for the coronation chair, whoever made it, were certainly influenced by the original setting of the Stone at Scone.

Nigel Tranter has drawn his version of the Stone and, thanks to his daring, we have a starting place for discussion. But Norman Atkinson believes the Stone would look rather different. Along with rock artist Rob Welsh, he committed his ideas to a replica which was exhibited for a time at Perth Museum.

If the Stone of Destiny did originate in the Holy Land, as we discussed in Chapter 5, it may well be composed of meteorite. If it came from Ireland or Iona, marble is the most likely material. Alternatively it may be basalt, black and polished with age. Least likely of all is sandstone.

Robert of Gloucester said Scota 'broghte into Scotland a whyte marble ston'. The throne of Charlemagne, which can still be seen at Aix-la-Chapelle in France, was white marble.

The old seals appended to charters of the Scottish kings give us pictorial evidence of what the Stone looked like. Made by highly skilled craftsmen, these were used over and over again on state documents. The makers would undoubtedly have been capable of producing good likenesses of the monarchs, just as coinminters give us a recognisable queen on our coins today. Artistic licence permitted the inclusion of items that had some symbolic significance to the king and to Scotland. The warrior king swashbuckles in his armour, riding a spirited horse and brandishing his sword on one surface, while on the other he is seated with great dignity on the Stone of Destiny which is bare, cushioned, or boxed.

Two seals are described as showing Edgar (1098-1107) 'sitting on a throne or rather stool of state; the legs terminating in eagle's claws' on charters in the Treasury of Durham Cathedral. There is another showing Alexander I 'sitting on a chair of state . . . under each hand, on the field of the seal, is a roundel charged with some indistinct figure'. This seal seems to have been the model for the designs of several later versions, such as those of David I and Malcolm IV. The seal of William the Lion shows 'The King seated on a chair or stool of state'.

The seal of Alexander II (1214-49) is of precisely the same design as that of William the Lion, but made in a more sophisticated style; the 'stool of state is more richly ornamented, and on each side is a branch of foliage'. He is 'Seated on a throne, decorated with rich pannels and four finials of fleur-de-lis . . . his feet resting on two lizards'.

John Balliol's seal is similar, showing him 'seated on a throne decorated with rich pannels and four crocketed pinnacles . . . on the dexter of throne is a shield, charged with an orle, the paternal arms of Balliol; on the sinister side is another, bearing a lion rampant'. There is another, said to have been used after Balliol's Great Seal was broken up, for his authority was still recognised in Scotland, on which the king sits on a throne, the arms and legs of which are the heads and feet of animals.

There is even a seal showing Edward I of England, undated. Under the title of 'Deputy Governor of Scotland' he is seated on a throne, his feet resting on two lions.

If any of these seating arrangements include an accurate representation of the Stone of Destiny, and if it did indeed disappear in 1296, then we should be able to discern some obvious change thereafter in the seals. We have descriptions of the seals of Robert the Bruce (1306–29). One is appended to a Melrose Charter, dated 1317: 'The King, sitting on a throne, decorated in the same style as that of Balliol'. Another dated 1320, shows Bruce 'seated on a throne or stool of state, the arms and legs of which are formed of the legs of an animal and the bodies and heads of serpents, placed transversely, and over them is thrown embroidered drapery'. Yet another shows him enthroned on 'a seat without back over which a draped cloth is thrown; the four corners of the seat are extended in the form of long curved necks and heads and legs of animals and the whole stands on a carved bracket'.

Tantalisingly, it comes down to interpretation. In general, it has been taken that the word 'stool' means the Stone of Destiny. As far as is known the term 'stool' has not normally been used in descriptions of other medieval coronation ceremonies. The word 'throne' refers to a wooden structure in which the Stone was contained. This was most beautifully carved, with see-through sections in the manner in which holy relics were sometimes held, because the Stone was accorded this degree of reverence and importance.

It is clear that a change of this sort did take place. The early kings sat quite comfortably on the Stone, with their knees forming a right-angle. Kings had to be of larger rather than smaller stature, as part of the physical image required of them, so these were relatively tall men. Even supposing they were only five feet eight inches, in order to sit like this the height of their seat would have to be seventeen inches (forty-three cm). In the later coronations the king is shown with his feet well above the ground, and he is considerably diminished in proportion to his throne. The little Stone of Scone is a mere eleven inches thick.

References to the items shown at the sides of the 'stool' are of interest. Alexander I's, David I's and Malcolm IV's have two round shield-like plaques. Alexander II's has what is described as a branch of foliage on either side. Balliol's seal has shields on each side.

The second feature of interest is the use of animal imagery. Edgar's 'stool' has legs terminating in eagle's claws, Alexander III rests his feet on two lizards and his 'stool' is ornamented with two lions' heads in cusped panels. The second Balliol seal shows the throne with animal heads and feet. Edward I rests his feet on two lions. Bruce's throne was 'decorated in the same style as that of Balliol, the arms and legs of which are formed of the legs of an animal, and the bodies and heads of serpents'. Interestingly, we also have the reappearance of the lizards last seen some fifty years earlier, well before the visit of Edward I.

As the Stone of Destiny moved through Scottish history it would collect decoration appropriate to each era of its existence. The Guinevere Stone at Meigle Museum is perhaps the best example of such a re-cycled monument. We can learn much about the type of decoration we might expect to find. First carved with cup-and-ring symbols between 2,000 and 500 BC, between the eighth to tenth centuries AD a 'ring of glory' filled with a cross was carved at the top, embellished with raised bosses thought to have been inspired by the rivet heads used in the art of metal-working jewellers. The rest of this face is taken up with animals, serpents and the figures of people now believed to carry some of the Arthurian story. The other side contains an iconography very popular in medieval central Scotland, that of Daniel in the Lion's Den. The stone was found this century, in use as a graveslab. In May 1991, after a life spent studying early manuscripts, Professor Norma Goodrich, a Californian historian, positively identified the Guinevere Stone as a reworked section from the triptych funeral-stone of King Arthur's queen, who is believed to have died nearby in the sixth century. Now it has pride of place in Meigle, near Coupar Angus, as a focus for tourists, art-lovers and historians.

The Stone we are looking for, then, stands at least 17 inches high, 18 inches deep and 32 inches wide. It is dark, polished, carved and painted with designs which include spirals, with a hollow in the top not unlike a footprint. It has traces of carved lettering probably in Latin, possibly in Gaelic, once picked out in red and white, or in which precious metal has been inlaid. There may be several other carvings, such as the Irish harp, a Pictish boar, Daniel and his lions. It has legs or feet like eagle's claws and, running up and down the front edges, the legs of animals, possibly lizards. On either side pairs of crook-shaped hooks were fixed so that it could be slung on two poles for transport.

Professor Cowan breathes fresh air and honest puzzlement: 'My own head's getting in a fankle about this Stone business.'

His main concern now is that much more research is needed into old documents. Legends are all very well, but 'I don't know where any of the inaugurations were held, from Kenneth Mac Alpin onwards, because I haven't looked. It seems to me this is something we should be paying more attention to. It's something for someone to do. What do we know about the inaugurations of these kings? Why is Scone so important? Scone is certainly big in the thirteenth century, but was it before? What's so significant about Scone? Why not Dunkeld? We know it was the centre in Kenneth Mac Alpin's time, and then later they shifted the centre to St Andrews. And if there was a Stone of Destiny, presumably it went to St Andrews along with the relics of Columba.

'We could start by scrutinising the documents to try and get a picture of what was thought about inaugurations in the medieval period up to Bruce, from all the sources, and see where that leads us. Comparative studies would be really interesting – Ireland seems to be better documented, as usual. Anglo-Saxon kings: how were they inaugurated? It wouldn't be easy – there's not a lot of information – but you might be able to infer certain things if you knew *where* people were inaugurated. Of course archaeology could help – the trouble is, what do you excavate? Scone Palace is built over the Abbey, which I understand was knocked down to build it.'

What would the Stone of Destiny look like? 'We know there's a big amalgam of different artistic traditions on the Pictish stones – they borrow from Ireland, they borrow from Anglo-Saxon England, the likelihood is that in matters of ritual they would probably borrow as well. We should be paying more attention to ritual sites in Scotland, because there must be others. People have had different ideas about this, but I don't know that we've ever really pursued them.'

What has he to say about the Stone newly arrived in Edinburgh? 'I wonder . . . How do you explain this nondescript lump? See, it doesnae even fit as a seat.'

Why does it matter? 'Edward stole the Stone as a deliberate

slight to the symbols of Scottish sovereignty. Every day and every hour that that Stone has remained at Westminster has been a slight to the Scottish sense of nationhood. If we use that argument, then we have an obligation to find out as much as we can about what the people themselves and the kings and the church thought about these symbols in the period up to 1296. And we haven't really done it. This matters very much – we need to know and understand about our roots and where we came from.

We have already noted in Chapter 17 how Walter Scott's love for Melrose Abbey was translated into his removal of some of the ancient stones for the building of Abbotsford. The stone that may have marked the grave of King Arthur, near that of his queen, was blown up and used as building material for Arthurstone House, not far from Meigle. Nineteenth-century builders, like others before them, thought nothing of cutting down ancient monoliths to suitable sizes for use in house-walls and foundations. In Forteviot, carved Pictish faces look out from the walls of several houses – who knows what lies hidden within other dwellings in that area? Chunks of the Counsel Table at Finlaggan may be found in drystane dykes or propping up Islay farmhouses and cattle sheds.

And what if, on your travels, you should find a likely-looking stone? Scotland, unlike England, has a particularly helpful system of dealing with Treasure Trove, aimed at protecting our material cultural heritage so that everyone can enjoy it, here. Any object whose original owner or rightful heir cannot be identified belongs to the Crown, which can opt to exercise its ownership rights. Accordingly, if you discover something of interest – a piece of jewellery, or an ancient carved marble stone – you should report it to the National Museum of Scotland in Edinburgh. If they decide to hold on to it you will be rewarded with its full market value, as happened with the famous St Ninian's Isle treasure forty years ago.

So it could be worth keeping an eye open wherever you travel in Scotland, leaving no stone unturned.

CHAPTER TWENTY-TWO

———————————— ≈ ————————————

FREEDOM COME-ALL-YE

N ow that the Stone of Scone has been returned to Scotland, where does it leave the story of the Stone of Destiny, and of what importance is it to Scotland? Having scrutinised the writings of antiquarians, listened to the legends, mulled over the myths and considered the pronouncements of academics, how do we feel about this symbol of the relationship between Scotland and England – and what does it matter as we approach the millennium? Perhaps the summing-up should be the thoughts and reactions of poets, novelists, song-writers, commentators, working historians and ordinary folk.

Robert Louis Stevenson (1850-94) wrote of the Scottish-English relationship: 'Here are two people almost identical in blood, language and religion, and yet a few years of quarrelsome isolation ... have so separated their thoughts and ways, that not unions, not mutual dangers, nor steamers nor railways, nor all the King's horses and all the King's men seem able to obliterate the broad distinction.'

Why do we not simply merge with England? What is it that convinces us we're different? For there is no such thing as 'Scottish blood' – on the contrary, the people who live in Scotland are a polyglot collection of immigrants who have been arriving here since the last Ice-age. It's something we share with the people of England. Why is it, then, that in spite of this and other links, in spite of all the efforts made over the centuries to unite these two nations through force, political union, joint monarchies, even advertising campaigns, there still seems to be such a desire for separateness prevalent in Scotland? And if the Scots do truly feel so disadvantaged, what is it that time and time again stops them from helping themselves to a Scottish parliament?

Colossal ignorance of our own history is one problem. We do not insist on the teaching of it in our schools. A little is permitted if there is a teacher available who happens to have an interest in the subject, but that is all. Young people come out of school totally unaware of their country's background. Instead, passively, we permit our understanding of ourselves to be peddled to us by the soft nostalgias of the tourist industry, moulded by the meagre requirements of an examination board.

Revolutions are rarely started by crowds of ordinary people, most of whom simply want to get on with their ordinary lives. Much more often changes are put into motion by small acts on the part of individuals. A vegetable seller called Jenny Geddes threw a stool at Dean Hannay in St Giles Cathedral on 23rd July 1637 and started a rebellion that ended with the decapitation of Charles I.

Four idealistic students started something when they brought the Stone home in 1951. The lives of many people were affected by their efforts, and most of them died before seeing them crowned with success.

Kay Matheson has no regrets about her hand in the affair, 'It affected my life – very much so. But it was important because it brought attention to the neglect of Scotland. Taking the Stone wakened the Scots people up a bit too. They're less apathetic now.'

Ian Hamilton, having successfully sold his books on the Stone-taking over the years, says he feels 'intensely proud that it was I who had that ambition. After all, to try and stir up your country to remind it that it has got a soul is a laudable ambition for any young man . . . Without any doubt the Scots are better than they were . . . Now, one could say, there is definitely a Scottish nation and a Scottish national culture . . . A nation that can survive without a government is a very real nation indeed. It's in our language, and in the way we approach problems – and of course I'm very conscious of it in the law. If people are daft enough to vote for one or other of the parties who want us to be governed four hundred miles away from the south east corner of the island, they deserve all they get.'

After the events of 1951, Hamilton's life zig-zagged between the legal profession and several others. He helped a friend, Kenny MacKenzie, set up Castle Wynd printers in Edinburgh in the 1950s, and published four volumes of Hugh MacDiarmid's poetry including *A Drunk Man Looks at the Thistle*, which he now describes as 'the proudest thing I have done with my life'. He wrote a prize-winning play about 'the Scots and their inability to cope with disaster in any other way than by singing romantic songs'. Now a well-known QC, he says, 'I'll die a pauper because I've always had something more interesting to do than put money away for my old age. I don't intend to have an old age anyway.'

Both Gavin Vernon and Alan Stuart ducked out of the limelight in the years that lay between the taking of the Stone and its legal return in November 1996, when they seemed glad enough to acknowledge the part they had played.

Bertie Gray had given everyone involved a crumb of the Stone as a memento. The tiny pieces of sandstone were set in rings, kiltpins, wrapped in old letters, hidden in desks, and left as heirlooms. Novelist Nigel Tranter keeps his beneath a tiny silver replica of the coronation chair. Author Naomi Mitchison, recalling 1951, says she considered hiding the Stone by putting it into Carradale river, 'where it would be among other stones . . . It was a good game of hide and seek while it lasted.' She agrees that 'what is supposed today to be the particular stone, may not be'.

Of what relevance were all these adventures – and who is now bothered about whether or not an old Stone of Destiny still exists, or that a non-representative person or group of people may secretly be holding in hiding an object of national interest? Judging by the constant stream of correspondence to newspapers and the media from all over the world, quite large numbers of people care passionately.

Some have always been prepared to take risks. Back in 1951, John Rollo decided he'd better find out exactly where he stood in relation to a certain hunk of sandstone hidden in his factory. He engaged a legal friend in casual discussion: 'Supppose someone received the Stone and looked after it, knowing nothing about its taking, was given it in Scotland and simply acted as a caretaker. If he was found in possession of it what would the charge be?' Quoth the lawyer: 'If he knew nothing of it, he was no party to the English charge of Sacrilege. If it could be proved that it was stolen property, and it was given to him in Scotland, then he was a re-setter in Scots law. But before a charge of re-set could be raised, ownership of the alleged Stone articles would have to be proved, and this would be the crux of the whole thing.' Rollo laughed. What right had the English Crown to possession?

Author Arnold Kemp, one-time Editor of the *Herald*, enlarged on this: 'It depends on whether you approach the question from a point of strict legality. Scotland's constitutional arrangements are governed by the Treaty of Union and its sovereignty is vested in the Union. UK sovereignty is said to reside in the monarch. London, on these grounds, can claim the Stone, which is of course the symbol of Scottish sovereignty. This, however, is carrying matters too far. The decision not to return the Stone to Scotland in the '50s . . . was one of several crass decisions that were taken around the time . . . Whatever the legality, the Stone belongs to Scotland spiritually and morally . . . The contemporary spirit of Scotland, I am sure, is that sovereignty resides with the people, as indeed it does in most democratic constitutions . . . The Stone, like other symbols of state, has significance because it gives material expression to the abstract concept of Scottish sovereignty and proof of the claim that Scotland remains a nation, though in Union with England. I was strongly of the opinion that the Stone should be returned to Scotland. From this you may guess that I support Home Rule!'

Invited to give their views on Stones in general, people

respond in different ways. The Prince of Wales, cheerfully prepared to pronounce on topics ranging from architecture to other people's car exhaust emissions, and who may one day have to sit athwart a Stone, like the queen, 'makes it a rule not to comment.' Donald Dewar MP is thoughtful; 'For myself the Stone is a symbol of the continuity of Scotland's history and a reminder of our stormy relationship with our neighbours in medieval times.'

New legends continue to germinate. A note arrives from an address in Bexhill-on-Sea: 'I was told about the Stone of Destiny fifty years ago when I was a child in Ireland. A king of Scotland demanded it of the High King of Ireland The latter being a wily man and not wishful to quarrel with his neighbour, who was probably stronger than him, cut a piece of black stone, had a mason carve a few runes on it, and sent it to Scotland. The true Stone of Destiny remains on the Hill of Tara to this day!' A letter comes from Ayrshire telling of a dark stone with a ring in it, built into the side of the Fairlieburn near Mary Queen of Scots bridge, and noting 'Ian Hamilton once lived in Fairlie for a while'. Most of the tales that turn up are garbled versions of the Matheson-Hamilton event, leavened with snatches of half-attended-to radio programmes and lumps of legend.

The Knights Templar hold on to their stone at Dull and talk of 'equations' and other stones. But when the one they delivered to the People's Palace in Glasgow in 1990 was examined, its very convincing-looking crack was found to have been chiselled carefully on only two surfaces – it did not go through the stone at all, which had never been broken. No trace of either bronze dowels nor of any other metal was found, proving conclusively that theirs is not the one mended by Bertie Gray. Ian Hamilton reinforced this when he said it was not the one he had taken from Westminster.

Looking back over the countless surviving legends about the Stone, it is tempting to ask what use it is to the people of Scotland to rake over the dead coals and the dying fires of national fervour, at a time when the whole of Britain is likely to disappear down the gullet of Europe? Of what possible relevance to Europe is the folklore of an apparently cowed and apathetic people dwelling on its northern fringes, and of what conceivable interest to the world at large? Rosalind Mitchison, Professor Emeritus of Social History at Edinburgh University, said, 'Well, you don't want to lose a species. The Scots *were* one of the earliest peoples of the world to express a feeling of nationality.' If nothing else, Scotland is a curiosity. Will her destiny join that of her vanishing stones – will she too fade out in a miasma of soap-opera, helpless moans and sentiment as she walks off hand in hand with England into the sunset of the British Empire?

Medieval historian Alexander Grant believes the Scottish perspective on European affairs is 'good for debunking English history in the eyes of the world'. So hard have Scottish historians had to work at discovering the roots of their civilisation, and so painstakingly have they done this, that they are now in demand to write the histories of other countries.

Bright new talent crops up. Dr Fiona Watson, Lecturer in History at Stirling University, who specialises in the fourteenth century and the Wars of Independence, says 'The Stone of Destiny – or the Stone of Scone – was the first unifying symbol of the new Scotland . . . the first literary description of it comes from a Yorkshire chronicler, Walter of Guisborough, after it was stolen. He says it was very large, concave and shaped like a round chair – which doesn't sound like the object that arrived in Edinburgh . . . A thousand years ago it stood for the creation of a new country. After it went to Westminster it became even more powerful, standing for a lost nationhood.' The Edinburgh ceremony 'was designed to show the equality of our relationship with England. Whatever you think of the intentions behind it, there must be a worry whether symbolism like this can still work in the age of the Internet. Or whether it is more likely to rebound . . . When no one could read or write, symbols were necessary. But today, when . . . the greatest of all national symbols – the monarchy – looks increasingly shaky, will the people buy it?'

To be conscious of our nationality is not to be exlusive. We all declare multiple allegiances. The fact that we enjoy being Scottish or Welsh or Bangladeshi does not exclude the possibility of our being a few other things too. We feel proud of being a Glaswegian, and that as such we are different from – and doubtless superior to – an Edinburger; the reverse is also true. We are more inclined to boast about being a Gael than a Lowlander, about being 'working class' than 'middle class'. We fuss about whether we're Scottish or British – the rest of the world, if they think of us at all, think we're English. And the more European we all become, the more we will need to feel firmly rooted in our own topography, history and genealogy, with all its folklore and traditions, stones and all.

What possible relevance could the Stone of Destiny have for the new Scots, people who have come to live here from other cultures? 'They've become part of a nation that's been in process of formation for about fifteen hundred years,' says Professor Cowan, 'and it's just as much in their interest to understand that as it is in ours.'

A suggestion turns up that the famous Sinclair family who, it is thought, sailed to Canada in the late fourteenth century, before Columbus, took the Stone of Destiny into hiding there.

Professor Cowan is sceptical: 'Honestly, I don't buy it. I did look into it at one time. It's not impossible, I have to say that, especially with the Sinclair interest in Orkney. Through Orkney I'm sure they acquired some knowledge of Orcadians being in the New World at the time of the Vikings. From the Vinland Sagas they must have known that the Vikings got to North America, so why shouldn't an Orcadian have got there? But by the early sixteenth century there was a great craze throughout Europe for writing or reviving any legends that seemed to suggest that their people had got to North America before Columbus so they could then put in a claim for a chunk of it. The Venetians, the Spanish, everybody was busily looking for anything in their archives that might suggest that they had a better claim. I think it's a myth. They claimed that they found some buildings in Nova Scotia showing evidence of Scottish building techniques. Ranald Nicholson, a very respected historian, thinks it's possible that the Sinclairs went to Nova Scotia – he leaves it open . . .'

For the moment, the story of the Stone of Destiny has to remain tantalisingly unfinished business. From the evidence we have collected from literal, artistic, scientific and other sources so far, it looks likely that Edward I was indeed duped back in 1296. The plain little sandstone lump in Edinburgh has merely been masquerading as the real thing down the years. But far older and more obscure treasures have been rediscovered.

If we are interested in finding the true Stone of Destiny, we need to keep our ears, our eyes and our minds open. On a practical level we need to encourage and fund much more research into our history, archaeology and ethnography. We need to stimulate an interest in these things in our children. We should value the keepers of the nation's memories, both sane and apparently crazy; the story-tellers, the traditionalists, the curious who go hunting details, dowsers, hill-walkers, farmers, the singers of songs, even the folk-dancers. For all we know, the clues we're looking for may be staring us in the face through their work.

The insights provided by the creative imagination have sparked off many a discovery and we should pay heed to them. Writers such as Nigel Tranter create a warmth of interest in Scottish History that no academic can do. New writers come forward – Andrew Greig is currently researching for a novel about the Stone. The Mystic Megs too have their uses, in prising open the closed doors of people's mind-sets. Until the historians, archaeologists, geographers, divers, geo-physicists, and working people find, as they will, new pieces of the jig-saw, the puzzle will have to remain temporarily unsolved, and an open verdict declared on the Stone of Destiny.

And, while we're searching for the Stone, what of the true destiny of Scotland? As things are, we behave like a person on the dole in that Catch-22 situation where we're frightened to risk the poorly paid job on offer for fear of losing benefits. Making our own decisions and living with the consequences, with no one to blame but ourselves for the bits that don't work – that's self-government. That's the freedom of being a fully developed nation. Nobody advocates pointless, bloody revolution, but finding the courage to move out from under England's protective shadow to take a look at what and who we really are at the end of the twentieth century is going to be essential if we want to change anything. It's not only a magic Stone we need. It's the bottle.

THE FREEDOM COME-ALL-YE

Roch the wind in the clear day's dawnin',
Blaws the cloods heelster gowdy ow'r the bay.
But there's mair nor a cauld wind blawin'
Through the great glen o' the warld the day.
It's a thocht that will gar oor rottans -
a' they rogues that gan gallus fresh and gay -
Ta' the road an' seek ither loanins
For their ill ploys tae sport an' play.

Nae mair will the bonnie callants
Mairch tae war, when oor braggarts crousely craw,
Nor wee weans frae pit-heid an' clachan
Mourn the ships sailin' doon the Broomielaw.
Broken faimlies in lands we've heirriet
Will curse Scotland the Brave nae mair, nae mair;
Black an' white, ane til ither mairriet
Mak' the vile barracks o' their maisters bare.

O come all ye at hame wi' freedom,
Never heed whit the hoodies croak for doom;
In your hoose a' the bairns o' Adam
Can find breid, barley bree an' painted room.
When Maclean meets wi's freens in Springburn
A' the roses an' geans will turn tae bloom,
And a black boy frae yont Nyanga
Dings the fell gallows o' the burghers doon.

         – Hamish Henderson.

CHRONOLOGY

DATE	EVENTS	LOCATION
*c.*2000 BC	Jacob dreams while asleep on his stone pillow – later it becomes the centre of the Temple at Jerusalem	ISRAEL
*c.*500 BC	Prophet Jeremiah rescues Princess + relics from Nebuchadnezzar	ISRAEL
*c.*500 BC	Jeremiah disappears + scribe + princess	EGYPT
c. 500 BC	Phoenicians sailing in Mediterranean and beyond.	SPAIN
c. 500 BC	Dan people land a prophet, a scribe and a princess in	IRELAND
55–54 BC	Caesar and Romans invade Britain	BRITAIN
AD 43	Romans begin conquest of Britain	BRITAIN
AD 122	Hadrian's Wall built	ENGLAND
AD 140–142	Antonine Wall built	SCOTLAND
500 BC-AD 400	Trading between the Mediterranean, Spain, Ireland and Britain	WHITHORN
c. AD 400	Boats sailing to Dalriada	DUNADD
AD 407	Romans leave Britain	
AD 432–61	St Patrick working as missionary	IRELAND

AD 537	King Arthur d.	SCOTLAND?
AD 563	Columba goes from Ireland to	IONA
AD 632	Death of Mohammed.	
c. AD 700	Vikings attack coasts Columba's relics taken from Iona to mainland	DUNSTAFFNAGE
AD 800	Charlemagne crowned Emperor	ROME
c. AD 800	Vikings still a threat. Kenneth MacAlpin takes St C.'s relics + Stone to And at some time later to	DUNKELD SCONE
11th Century	Macbeth crowned on Stone	SCONE
till 1296	Stone of Destiny in use	SCONE
1296	A Stone is taken by Edward I to Westminster and used till 1950 for coronations.	LONDON
13th century	A Stone may have been hidden	DUNSINANE
14th century	A Stone may have been taken by Macdonalds of Islay	FINLAGGAN
17th century	A Stone may have gone from Islay to mainland or island with the Campbells	SKYE
1818	A stone found in Macbeth's Castle	DUNSINANE
1950	A Stone taken to Scotland from Westminster Abbey	STIRLING
1951	A Stone is left at	ARBROATH
1951	A stone is taken to Westminster	LONDON
1965	A stone turns up in Parliament Square	EDINBURGH

1965	A stone is taken into safe-keeping by Knights Templar	DUNDEE
1970s	A seer is shown two Stones	PERTHSHIRE
1972	A stone is dedicated at a Dundee church	DUNDEE
1989	George Wyllie makes some 'Carry-out Stones'	GOUROCK
1991	The Knights Templar Stone re-housed	DULL
1990s	Archaeologists continue to search for Stone of Destiny	SCOTLAND
1996	Stone of Scone is lent to Scots, handed over at Edinburgh Castle.	EDINBURGH

SOURCES

1. CARRIED AWAY AT CHRISTMAS
Ian Hamilton, *A Sense of Treason* (Lochar, 1990); Ian Hamilton, *The Taking of the Stone of Destiny* (Lochar, 1991); *Glasgow Herald; Scotsman.*

2. THE HOSTAGE STONE
Ian Hamilton, *A Sense of Treason* (Lochar, 1990); Wendy Wood, *Yours Sincerely for Scotland* (Barker, 1970); BBC recording of John Rollo; *Glasgow Herald; Scotsman; Arbroath Herald.*

3. KINGS, QUEENS AND CORONATION CHAIRS
Westminster Abbey Official Guide (Dean & Chapter of Westminster, 1988); Professor William Skene, *The Coronation Stone* (Edinburgh, 1869); Wendy Wood, *Yours Sincerely for Scotland* (Barker, 1970); A. Smyth, *Warlords and Holy Men: Scotland AD 80–1000* (London 1894); Charles J. Burnett & Christopher J. Tabraham, *The Honours of Scotland* (Historic Scotland, 1993).

4. HOW THE LEGENDS BEGAN
Duncan Williamson, *Fireside Tales of the Traveller Children* (Canongate, 1983); Jennifer Westwood, *Albion* (Collins, 1985); Professor William Skene, *The Coronation Stone* (Edinburgh 1869); Dominica Legge, *Scottish Historical Review*, Vol. XXXVIII, pp. 109–13, Archie McKerracher, *Scots Magazine*, December 1984, August 1989; Marion Campbell, *Argyll the Enduring Heartland* (Turnstone Books, 1977); Alexander Fraser, *Lochfyneside* (St Andrew Press, 1971).

5. JACOB AND THE THUNDER STONES
Diane W. Darst, *Western Civilization* (New York, 1990); Eldon Rutter, *The Holy Cities of Arabia* (New York, 1918); E. Raymond Capt, *Jacob's Pillar* (Archaeological Institute of America, 1977); King James VI translation of the Bible.

6. IRELAND
Ward Rutherford, *Celtic Mythology* (Aquarian Press, 1897); Peter Harbison, *Pre-Christian Ireland* (Thames & Hudson, 1988); R.A.S. Macalister (ed.), *Lebor Gabala Erenn* (Irish Texts Society, 1920--, vols 34, 35, 39, 41, 44); *Times Atlas of World History* (Guild, 1989 edn); F. Marian McNeill (ed.), *An Iona Anthology* (New Iona Press, 1991).

7. ROMANS AND CHRISTIANS
Peter & Fiona Somerset Fry, *History of Scotland* (Routledge, 1985); Janet B. Christie, *Scots Magazine*, November 1970; Andrew R. M. Patterson, *A Celtic Saga* (St Andrew Press, 1991); Peter Hill & Dave Pollock, *The Whithorn Dig* (Whithorn Trust, 1991); Peter Hill, *Whithorn 3, Excavations* (1990); *Guidebook to Melrose Abbey* (1888); *Melrose Abbey* (HMSO, 1990); Geoffrey Stell, *Exploring Scotland's Heritage, Dumfries & Galloway* (Royal Commission on the Ancient and Historic Monuments of Scotland, 1986); A.A.M. Duncan, *Scotland, the Making of a Kingdom* (Oliver & Boyd, 1978).

8. DALRIADA AND THE ROYAL BOAR
Graham Ritchie & Mary Harman, *Exploring Scotland's Heritage, Argyll & the Western Isles* (Royal Commission on the Ancient and Historic Monuments of Scotland, 1985); Ronald W.B. Morris, *The Prehistoric Rock Art of Argyll* (Dolphin, 1977); A.A.M. Duncan *Scotland, the Making of a Kingdom* (Oliver & Boyd, 1978).

9. COLUMBA, KING OF STORMS
E. Mairi MacArthur, *Iona, the Living Memory of a Crofting Community* (EUP, 1990); E. Mairi MacArthur, *Columba's Island* (EUP, 1995); E. Mairi MacArthur, *Iona* (Colin Baxter Island Guides, 1997); W. Reeves (ed.), *Life of Columba* (1884); Ian Finlay, *Columba* (Richard Drew, 1990); Ian Adamsom, *The Cruthin* (Pretani, 1986); P.A. MacNab, *Islands* (David & Charles, 1987); Fiona Macleod, *Iona* (Floris, 1982); F. Marian McNeil (ed.), *An Iona Anthology* (New Iona Press, 1991); *Proceedings of the Society of Antiquaries of Scotland*, Vol. 12, 1854.

10. DUNSTAFFNAGE
Graham Ritchie & Mary Harman, *Exploring Scotland's Heritage, Argyll & the Western Isles* (Royal Commission on the Ancient and Historic Monuments of Scotland, 1985); W. Douglas Simpson, *Dunstaffnage Castle and the Stone of Destiny* (Edinburgh, 1958); Nigel Tranter, *Kenneth* (Hodder, 1990); Lorn MacIntyre, *Scots Magazine*, June 1990.

11. SCOTLAND UNITED
A.A.M. Duncan, *Scotland, the Making of a Kingdom* (Oliver & Boyd, 1978); Croft Dickinson, revised A.A.M. Duncan, *Scotland from the Earliest Times to 1603* (Oxford 1977); Peter & Fiona Somerset Fry, *History of Scotland* (Routledge, 1985); Michael Lynch, *Scotland, A New History* (Century, 1991); *The Story of Scotland* (*Sunday Mail*, 1988); Nigel Tranter, *Kenneth* (Hodder, 1990).

12. WHO OWNS SCOTLAND
E.W. Robertson, *Scotland Under Her Earliest Kings*, Vol. III (1862); James Ferguson, *Alexander III* (McLehose, 1937); Jasper Ridley, *The History of England* (Routledge, 1981); Peter & Fiona Somerset Fry,

History of Scotland (Routledge, 1985); Wendy Wood, *Yours Sincerely for Scotland* (Barker, 1970); Stewart Ross, *Monarchs of Scotland* (Lochar, 1990).

13. ENGLAND'S EDWARD AND THE CELTIC FRINGES

R.J. Cootes, *The Middle Ages* (Longman, 1972); Valerie E. Chancellor, *Medieval and Tudor Britain* (Penguin, 1978); Nigel Tranter, *The Story of Scotland* (Routledge, 1987); Jasper Ridley, *The History of England* (Routledge, 1981); Nigel Tranter, *The Bruce Trilogy* (Hodder, 1971–2); Domenica Legge, *Scottish Historical Review*, Vol. XXXVIII, pp.109–13; *Scots Magazine*, November 1970.

14. ROBERT THE BRUCE

A.A.H Douglas (ed.), *John Barbour* (McClellan, 1964); Geoffrey Barrow, *Robert the Bruce and the Scottish Identity* (Saltire Society, 1984); Jasper Ridley, *The History of England* (Routledge, 1981); Ronald McNair Scott, *Robert the Bruce* (Canongate, 1982); Nigel Tranter, *The Bruce Trilogy* (Hodder, 1971–2); *The Story of Scotland* (*Sunday Mail*, 1988).

15. THE STONE OF SKYE

Norman Newton, *Islay* (David & Charles, 1988); Ronald Williams, *The Lords of the Isles* (Chatto & Windus, 1984); Domhnall MacEacharna, *The Lands of the Lordship* (Argyll, 1976); Norman Macdougall, *James IV* (John Donald, 1989); David Caldwell, *Finlaggan Interim Report and Update* (National Museums of Scotland, 1991); R.W. Munro, *Monro's Western Isles of Scotland* (Edinburgh & London, 1961), edn of Dean Monro's 'Description'; Roger Miket & David L. Roberts, *The Medieval Castles of Skye and Lochalsh* (MacLean, 1990); *Ceannas Nan Gaidheal* (Clan Donald Lands Trust, 1985).

16. THE KNIGHTS TEMPLAR

Ian B. Cowan, P.H.R. Mackay & Alan Macquarrie (eds), *Knights of St John of Jerusalem in Scotland* (Scottish History Society, Edinburgh 1983); Archie McKerracher, *Scots Magazine*, June 1991, p.261.

17. SIR WALTER SCOTT AND EDINBURGH CASTLE

Jane Porter, *Scottish Chiefs* (Routledge, 1857, edn); Sir Walter Scott, *Tales of A Grandfather* (1828, 1829; Samuel Johnson & James Boswell, *A Journey to the Western Islands of Scotland*, ed. R.W. Chapman (OUP, 1970); *Edinburgh Castle* (HMSO, 1966, 1989); *Guide to Abbotsford*; *Proceedings of the Society of Antiquaries of Scotland*, vols 4 and 100.

18. MACBETH'S CASTLE

Seton Gordon, *Highways and Byways in the Central Highlands* (Macmillan, 1948); James Myles, *Rambles in Forfarshire* (Dundee, 1850); Robert Chambers, *Pictures of Scotland* (1828); Alexander Hutcheson, *Old Stories in Stone* (Dundee, 1927); Archie McKerracher, *Perthshire in History and Legend* (John Donald, 1988); Sir H.E.

Maxwell, *The Early Chronicles Relating to Scotland* (McLehose, 1912); Ian C. Hannah, *The Story of Scotland in Stone* (Oliver & Boyd, 1934); George Ritchie, *Stones of Destiny* (Kirk Session, Scone, 1986); *Statistical Accounts of Scotland*, 1798, 1857; *Scots Magazine* May 1954, November 1975, December 1984, August 1989; *Minutes of the Society of Antiquaries of London*, Vol. XXXIV, 1817–23; *Proceedings of the Society of Antiquaries of Scotland* 1857, 1869; *The Times*, 1 January 1819; *London Morning Chronicle*, January–February 1819; *Edinburgh Evening Chronicle*, January–February 1819; *Caledonian Mercury*, 7 January 1819; *Inverness Courier*, 27 February 1951; Lady Pamela Mansfield, paper on 'Scone and the Stone of Destiny'.

19. A ROYAL PECULIAR
Wendy Wood, *Yours Sincerely for Scotland* (Barker, 1970); *Daily Telegraph*, 23 October 1974.

20. BACK TO THE FUTURE
July–December 1996; *Herald, Independent, Scotsman, Scotland on Sunday, The Times*.

21. THE STONE OF DESTINY
Ian Finlay, *Columba* (Richard Drew, 1990); Ruth & Vincent Megaw, *Early Celtic Art* (Shire, 1986); Sue Youngs (ed.), *The Work of Angels* (British Museum, 1989); *The Book of Kells* (Thames & Hudson, 1980); *Dark Age Sculpture* (National Museum of Antiquities of Scotland, 19xx); Anna Ritchie, *Picts (Historic Buildings and Monuments, 1989); Nigel Tranter's Scotland* (Richard Drew, 1981); Descriptive Catalogue of the Great Seals and Signets of the Kings of Scotland in Register House, Edinburgh; Ian C. Hannah, *Story of Scotland in Stone* (Oliver & Boyd, 1934).

22. FREEDOM COME-ALL-YE
Eric Macdonald Lockhart, Counsellor at Law, *A Scheme of Home Rule with Reference to Scotland* (Glasgow, 1886).

GENERAL
Christopher Haig (ed.), *Cambridge Historical Encyclopedia of Great Britain and Ireland*; Alfred W. Crosby, *Ecological Imperialism: the Biological Expansion of Europe 900–1900* (CUP, 1986); Norman Stone (ed.), *Times Atlas of World History* (Guild, 1989, 3rd edn); Magnus Magnusson (ed.); *The Nature of Scotland* (Canongate, 1991); *Touring Map of Scotland* (Geographica); *Ordnance Survey Pathfinder Series* and *Landranger Series* of maps (Southampton); HMSO guidebooks to various castles; Anthony New, *A Guide to the Abbeys of Scotland* (London, 1988).

INDEX

Abbotsford 181, 135
Adamnan 63, 68, 69, 71, 72, 76
Aelfred the Great of Wessex 90
Agricola 53
Alberactus 35
Alexander I, king of Scots 176, 178
Alexander II, king of Scots 59, 92, 100, 177, 178
Alexander III, king of Scots 26–28
Alien Act 1705 95
Alnwick castle 92
Andrew of Wyntoun 30
Angus I, king of Picts 67, 175
Annan 163
Anne, Queen 94, 95
Antonine wall 54, 55
Arbroath abbey 18, 19, 92, 114, 162, 175
Armadale castle 124
Arthur, king 181
Arthurstone House 159, 181
Athelstan 90
Attlee, Clement 21
Avienus 51

Baldwin II, king 129
Balliol, John 101–2, 103, 104, 108, 177, 178
Bandirrann 149
Bannockburn, battle of 87, 93, 113, 117, 130

Barbour, John 100, 109, 131
Baruch, a scribe 45, 46, 47
Bede, the Venerable 56, 58
Beregonium, lost city of 81, 83
Berwick 103, 107, 112
Bisset, Baldred, Canon of St Andrews 28, 35, 38
Black Rood of St Margaret 60, 137
Black Stone (in University of Glasgow) 55
Blain, Jimmie, Custodian of Melrose abbey 60
Boece, Hector 37, 81
Boniface VIII, Pope 35, 36
Book of Deer 171
Book of Durrow 175
Book of Kells 175
Boswell, James 134
Brander, pass of 87
Braveheart 107, 169
Brec/Brech, Simon 32, 39, 47, 50
Brian Boru 15, 51
Bridei mac Maelchon, king of Picts 71, 72
Brith (journal) 14
Broichan, Bridei's tutor 71
Brown, Revd Thomas 145
Bruce, Robert 24, 27, 30, 38, 58, 59, 80, 93, 102, 107–117, 118, 120, 130, 131, 177
   excommunicated 113;

heart of 60, 116, 163;
throne of 178
Buchan, earl of 112
Burns, Robert 95, 134

Cambuskenneth abbey 115
Camerarius, David 81
Campbell, Angus Peter 167

Canmor/Caenmor, Malcolm
35, 91, 94, 116
Carn Cul re Eirinn 70
Carrick, earl of, see Bruce,
Robert
Castle Urquhart 71
Cauldron of Dagda 48
Celtic Stone 133
Cenel Loairnn, fortress of 82
Charlemagne 23, 176
Charles I 151, 183
Chronicle of Lanercost 154
Chronicle of Melrose 59
Church of St Columba,
Lochee 131–2
Churchill, Winston 21
Clachan Brath (Judgement Day
Stones) 75
Clement V, pope 130
Coldstream 40, 163, 164, 165
Columba see St Columba
Comgall 64
Comyn, John 107, 108, 109,
112, 113
Constantine 56, 84, 86, 90
Cooldrevne, battle of 69
Coronation Chair 32, 74, 111,
154, 155, 167
Coronation Stone 1, 153, 160
Corpus Christi College,
Cambridge 105–6, 127
Counsel Stone 123
Craig Phadrig, hillfort 71, 175
Cromwell, Oliver 25, 93, 151
Cruithnechan, a priest 69
Crusades 98, 118, 115

Cuthbert, prior of Lindisfarne
59

Dal Riata 64, 65, 67
Dalriada, ancient kingdom of
25, 53, 62, 63, 70, 72, 73,
79, 81, 85, 86, 161
Dan, tribe of 45, 46, 48
David I, king of Scotland 91,
129, 177, 178
David II, king of Scotland 27,
61
David, king of Judah 44, 45
de Montfort, Simon 97, 98
Declaration of Arbroath 114,
115, 163
Diormit, Columba's attendant
71, 72
Don, Dr A.C., Dean of
Westminster 13, 21
Douglas, James 110, 116, 118
Duan of Alba, the 84
Dubh, Domhnall 123
Dumbarton 64, 113
Dunadd 25, 62, 63, 65, 66, 67,
81, 83, 85, 86, 87, 161, 175
Dunaverty 64, 118
Dunfermline abbey 116, 117
Dunivaig castle 120
Dunkeld 73, 79, 81, 86, 88
Dunstaffnage 118
Dunollie 64, 82, 83
Dunsinnan 142, 143, 144, 146,
147, 159
Dunsinnan Stone 149
Dunstaffnage castle 79,
80, 82, 88
Durham cathedral 61, 176

Edgar, king of Wessex 90,
176, 178
Edinburgh castle 60, 104, 137,
138, 151, 161, 163, 172
Edward I, king of England xi,
1, 23, 25, 26, 27, 28, 30,

32, 33, 35, 36, 38, 39, 59, 60, 90, 93, 97, 98–106, 108, 109, 110, 113, 137, 138, 142, 148, 150, 151, 154, 160, 162, 163, 167, 177, 178, 180, 189
Edward II 105, 113, 114
Edward III, seal of 106
Edward the Confessor 157
Eilean Mòr 121, 122
Eithne, mother of Columba 68, 82, 83, 88
Eleanor, Queen of England, wife of Edward I 97, 101
Elizabeth, queen 151, 152
Elizabeth, Robert Bruce's queen 112, 113, 115
Enlightenment, the 96, 142
Ergadia, Ewen de 82
Evonium 81

Falls of Lora 83
Fergus, king of Dalriada 81, 137
Fingal, king 81
Finlaggan 120, 121, 122, 123, 181
Flodden, battle of 164
Fordun, John 32, 37, 120
Forsyth, Michael, Secretary of State for Scotland 1, 160, 163, 166, 167, 168, 170, 172, 177
Forteviot 88, 89, 181

Gabran 64
Gaidelon, 34
Gartan 69
Gaythelus 31–2, 39
Geddes, Jenny 183
George VI, king, 12, 13, 21, 151
Giraldus 123
Glasgow University 4, 9, 13
Gray, Robert (Bertie) 2, 4, 9,

11, 15, 17, 19, 154, 162, 184, 186
Great Cause, the 101
Greyfriars Kirk 113
Guinevere Stone 179

Hadrian's Wall 84
Hamilton, duke of 152
Hamilton, Ian 1, 3, 4, 6, 7, 8, 10, 11, 16, 20, 21, 132, 155, 163, 170, 183, 184, 186
Hammurabi, king of Babylon 44
Hannay, Dean 183
Harbison, Peter 49
Hemingford, Walter 36
Henry II, king of England 92
Henry IV, king of England 25
HMS *Newcastle* 169
Hogg, James 139
Holy Island 101
Holyrood House 151, 169
Honours of Scotland 137, 151, 167
Houses of Parliament 156
Hunterian Museum 55

inauguration 102, 122
Inverasdale 12, 16
Iogenan 72
Iona 53, 59, 68, 70, 74, 78, 79, 80, 123, 176
IRA 156
Isabel, countess of Buchan 112
Islay 120

Jackson, Charles d'Orville Pilkington, sculptor 117
Jacob, grandson of Abraham 41, 42, 43, 73
Jacob's Pillar 45; Jacob's Pillow 38, 41, 58
James IV 127, 152
Jeremiah, prophet 45, 46, 47
Josselyn, Johnny 9

Kells 79
Kenneth II 90
Kent 8, 9
Kerr, William, Detective
   Inspector 16, 17–18
Kilchurn castle 76
Killiecrankie, battle of 131
Knights Templar 61, 128,
   129–33, 162, 186

Lamberton, Bishop William
   110, 111, 114, 130
Langholm 163
Latinus Stone 175
Leabhar Gabhala (Book of
   Invasions and Conquests) 47
Lewis Chessmen 154, 171
Lia Fail (Oracle Stone) 47, 49,
   50, 52, 53, 70, 161
Lindisfarne 58, 59, 101, 175
Llywelyn 99
Loch Awe School (masons) 130
Loch Etive 83
Loch nam Uamh 128
Lora, Ben 81
Lords of the Isles 74, 122

Mac Alpin, Kenneth 53, 57,
   65, 73, 79, 82, 83, 85, 86,
   88, 89, 108, 125, 180
Macbeth's Castle 38, 140–50
MacDiarmid, Hugh 2, 4, 184
Macdonald of Ardgay, Sweyn,
   a seer 132
Macdonald of Sleat, Sir Iain
   Bosville 130
Macdonalds of Skye 124, 128
Macdonald, Alexander, of
   Islay 107
MacDougall, John, of Lorn
   118, 119
McDuff, earl of Fife 112
MacLean, Sorley 168, 170
MacRae, Duncan 2
Maelrubha, a missionary 81

Maid of Norway 100
Malcolm I 90
Malcolm II 91
Malcolm IV 177, 178
Margaret, queen of Scots, wife
   of Alexander III 91, 100
Margaret, Saint 116
Marmone Stuhl (marble
   chair) 23
Marmorea cathedra (marble
   chair) 32
Mary, Queen of Scots 93
Matheson, Kay 3, 4, 6, 7, 8, 9,
   12, 16, 20, 128, 155, 168,
   170, 183
Meigle 175, 179
Mel Gibson 167
Melrose abbey 58, 59, 60,
   115, 131
Melrose Charter 177
meteorites 41, 42, 176
Molaisi, Saint 69
Monipennie, John 82
Mons Graupius, battle of 54
Montrose 103, 175
Monymusk Reliquary 73, 86,
   87
Mull 70, 118

Nairne, T.M. 144, 145,
   146, 149
Napoleon 134
Nennius xiv
Nevill's Cross, battle of 61
Nimmo, Revd John Mackay
   18, 20, 131, 162
Norham, Council of 101
Nuadaa, king of Ireland 48

Og, Angus, of the Isles 38,
   115, 116, 118, 120, 122,
   123, 129
Ogham script 52, 64, 66, 84
Ollam Fodhla, prophet 47, 50
Omphalos Stone 51

Ora Maritima 51

Paris, Matthew, chronicler 97
Parliament Square, Edinburgh 131
Patrick, St 67
Pennant, Thomas xii–xiii, xiv, 82
Philip IV of France 102, 130
Phoenicians 45–7, 63
Pictish Chronicle 73
Pictish Stone 133
Pictish symbols 84, 177, 180, 181
Picts 36, 39, 53, 54, 64, 66, 84, 85, 87
Pillar Stone, 44
Pius, Antoninus 54
Playfair, Dr James 143, 145
Pococke, Bishop 82
Polo, Marco 98
Poppleton Manuscript 127
Port a Churaich 70

Rathlin Island 118
regalia of Scotland 104
Reuda/Riata 64
Richard I, king of England 92
Robert I, see Bruce, Robert
Robert II 30, 93
Robert of Gloucester, monk 30
Rollo, John 12, 15, 16, 17, 18, 20, 160, 185
Rosslyn chapel 133
Roxburgh castle 112

St Aidan 58
St Andrews 88, 180
St Columba xiv, 53, 68–78, 82, 86, 154, 175, 180
    relics 79; 'St Columba's Pillow' 74; 'St Columba's Seat' 133
St Giles Cathedral 152, 161, 169, 183

St Ninian's cave 56; isle 181; shrine 57, 58, 115
Scalacronica 31
Scone 110, 112, 132, 137, 142, 150, 180
    abbey 30, 38, 85, 90, 104; palace 141, 180
Scota, daughter of Pharoah xiv, 31, 34, 36, 39, 50
Scotichronicon 31
Scott, Michael, wizard 60
Scott, Sir Walter 96, 134–9, 181
Scotti, the 52, 55, 79, 84
Scottish Covenant 3, 4
Sheila of Auchindell 119
Sinclair, Jamie, Laird of Dunsinnan 148, 150
Skene, William 31, 36, 64, 73
Sleat 124
Solomon 44
Solomon's Temple 129
Somerled 82
Song of Lewes 97
Standing Stones of Drumtrodden 56
Stanley, Dean of Westminster 73
'Stella Templum' 133
Stevenson, Robert Louis 182
Stirling 103, 107
Stirling castle 161
Stone of Destiny xi passim
Stuart, Alan 3, 4, 6, 8, 9, 16, 155, 170, 184
Sueno's stone 23, 175
Swinton, Major–Gen. Sir John 166
Sword of Nuada 48

Tacitus, Cornelius 53, 54
Tara 32, 37, 47, 49, 50, 53, 69
Tea, Princess, daughter of Zedekiah 45, 46, 47, 50

'Toom Tabard' 102
Tor Abb 71
Tower of London 112
Tranter, Nigel 2, 82, 83, 87, 110, 111, 116, 176, 184, 189
travellers 9–10
Treaty of Birgham 100
Turnberry castle 107
Turoe Stone 51

Union of Crowns, 1603 151
Urbicus, Lollius 54

Vernon, Gavin 3, 4, 6, 8, 9, 16, 155, 170, 184
Victoria, Queen 37, 96, 138
Vikings 79, 84, 188
Wallace, William 38, 39, 107, 161
Walter of Durham 105
Walter of Guisborough 187
Walter the Painter 104, 106
weaponry 130–1
Westminster abbey 1, 4, 6, 18, 19, 25, 38, 104, 112, 134, 138, 154, 155, 156, 159, 163, 164, 187
Poets' corner 6; Confessor's chapel 6
Whithorn 57, 58, 61, 115, 175
William of Rishanger 30
William the Conqueror 91
William the Lion 92
Williamson, Duncan, traveller xv, 29
Wishart, Bishop 110, 111
Wood, Wendy 4, 14–15, 18, 20, 152, 153
Wright, Canon Kenyon 170
Wyllie, George xiii, 168

Yolande of Dreux, Alexander III's queen 100

Zadok 24, 44
Zebulun, son of Jacob 43
Zedekiah, king of Jerusalem, 45